A Time to Remember

A Time to Remember

A WWII Evacuee's Childhood in Wales

Beryl Mathias

Dolbadau Road Press

All rights reserved. No part of this book may be reproduced, stored in a retrieval system, or transmitted, in any form or by any means, electronic, mechanical, photocopying, recording or otherwise without permission from Dolbadau Road Press, P.O. Box 363, Basye, Virginia, 22810 USA.
E-mail: DolbadauRoadPress@gmail.com

Cover photo: A farm in the eastern Preseli Hills of Wales by Andrea Sutcliffe

Back cover: British government poster concerning the evacuation of children to the countryside, 1939

Copyright © 2014 Beryl Mathias

ISBN-13: 978-1500683825
ISBN-10: 1500683825

About the Author

Beryl Mills Mathias was born in 1930 in Kent, England. In September 1939, she was among the first of more than three million children evacuated from English cities during World War II to protect them from German air raids.

She spent much of her childhood in rural West Wales, living with people not related to her in any way. At war's end, she was a young woman of 15 — and an orphan. Under the rules of the evacuation, she had to be sent back to her home town in England, even though she had no immediate family left there.

Her life after the war did not become any easier until she met and married Idris Mathias of Cardigan, Wales, while visiting friends there in 1950. Today the couple still live in Cardigan, near their five children.

The stories in this book are true; however, some of the names have been changed.

Handwritten annotations:

1939 DORATHY Sent to Wales with my school. Also my two brothers Jim + John. Grue up in Wales. Lovely life. MRS JAMES. Took care of us - ON THE FARM.

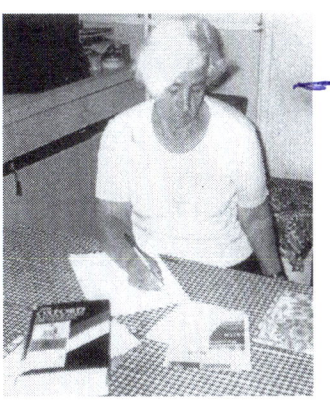

BERYL MATHIAS

MY NAME DOROTHY

I DID NOT whant To Leave WALES. My SISTeR Tock Me BACK To Londen at the end of the ware. IT Wash not a god Life for Me in Landen. I went To schote with to meny Buris. My SISTeR was to handy with wacking me. Tacken away and ENDY up at a ~~Convent~~ CONVENT ~~it wese~~. Haverford ~~wes~~ WEST w Had a LOVELY LIVE LEARNT a LOT. MADE me a good ~~person~~ PERSON

Chapter 1

My birth was a difficult one. I was sickly baby who needed a blood transfusion, with a fifty-fifty chance of survival. And against the odds I did! But was my survival the harbinger of the endless heartbreaks yet to come?

I was one of four children of Harold and Blanche Mills. Early on, things did not fare well for the family. When I was barely three years old, a terrible illness hit my sister Rosie and me. We were quickly admitted to the Bow Arrow Isolation Hospital, suffering from the dreaded diphtheria.

It was an awful place, stinking of all sorts of medical disinfectants and harsh treatment day and night. Rosie was a few beds from me, and one day there was a dreadful urgency by the nurses and the doctor around her bed.

I watched her die. I so much wanted to be at her bedside and hold her hand, but the blankets were over her and they took her away; it was not to be. And only a day before I saw her throw things off her bed—in play, I thought. But she was struggling for breath.

When she died, my entire world seemed to end. I fearfully alone had to battle the diphtheria. My parents came to visit me, dressed in white medical gowns with slits for their eyes. How they feared I would follow Rosie to the grave. It was a heart-breaking time for them.

The endless smelly torture swabs in and out of my throat left horrible scars on my neck. The stay there made me feel like a stranger to myself. Finally they let me go home. I had survived that horrible sickness. But the once easy atmosphere at home was gone; there was constant mourning, with hardly a word spoken, leaving me to feel like an outcast.

Our family troubles were far from being over. Two years later, Father fell seriously ill. I was at his side watching him suffer from terrible head pains and roll about on the floor with no relief. Mum was in a panic—what next to do to help him?

He was helped upstairs and put into his bed. He had the worst of ills, meningitis, the most painful affliction imaginable. He kept rolling off the bed and Mum had to keep pushing to stop him tumbling. I tried to help her, but tears of despair streamed from her eyes; she knew there was nothing to be done that would help or cure him.

He began dying in our arms and was eventually taken to the West Hill Hospital, where he passed away a few hours later. I attended his funeral and watched as his coffin was laid in the same grave as Rosie's. It was bitter blow to our already mourning family.

Life at home was quiet as the morgue, and every passing day tumbled on in an atmosphere of dread. But it was not to be over for us; another tragedy would soon tear our family apart. The Second World War was declared on Sunday, September 3, 1939. For me it meant a further onslaught of misery and our family divided.

First there was the anxiety and tension waiting for something to happen. Then within days we learned that my brother Freddie and I were to be evacuated — for our own safety, they said. My emotions were in turmoil. I seemed to suffer one unpleasant experience after another. My future was uncertain. That essential feeling of belonging, which is so important in childhood, was soon gone. I had no idea what a normal life should be.

Losing Rosie and Father and now Mum! My only stability had been Mum, and the thought of being without her was breaking my heart. Inside I was dying, life was discoloured, sensibility dimmed. I was terribly nervous and more fearful and miserable than ever.

Mum took us to the embarkation centre on Sunday following the Declaration. There were dozens of children with prominent labels displayed on their coats, carrying gas masks and bags or suitcases. A bus was waiting to transport us to areas considered safe from enemy bombing. We joined the noisy crowd.

I was very nervous in the hustle and bustle, and fear had me by the throat. I was trembling all over as Mum held me. I put my arms tight about her, tighter than ever before. 'Please, Mum I don't want to leave you.' I searched her eyes for a sign she might weaken and take us hack home.

But all I heard was, 'You will write as often as you can, you know this parting is for your own safety and Freddie's.' I refused to let her go, but soon I had to take my place beside Freddie. There was a sickness in my heart to think of being far away from Mum. We were bosom pals with no secrets between us, and somehow I knew there would be no journey home for me. We had been two of a kind.

Through all her losses, she had never lost hope until this parting shattered our lives. As I relive those uncertain moments in my mind, I feel I am talking to myself in a dream world. I never trusted my elder sister. I thought she was a scheming bitch who talked Mum into sending us away. (Later, she showed her dark sneaky colours by enlisting in the army, leaving Mum all alone to fend for herself. Had I known what she was up to, I would never have left home, no matter what.)

As the bus rumbled through the pastoral countryside, I recalled our last moments. 'What about your safety, Mum?' She said nothing, and with tears helped me into the bus, where I took my seat next to Freddie. She kissed us both farewell, then went outside and kissed her fingers and pressed them against the window. We did the same, and with bitter sadness in her eyes she joined the other parents.

Everywhere I saw a panic of goodbyes. Slowly, the cumbersome bus groaned away from the sea of distraught faces. I caught a final glimpse of Mum, a wave, and then she was gone.

Fearful children, realising for the first time what was happening to them, screamed and shouted and struggled to reach the door to get out. The panic was infectious, and the teachers who accompanied us tried hard to gain control.

'You are going to the seaside on week's holiday, then you'll be coming home,' one teacher said. A few enraged children fought her tooth and nail, even throwing gas masks in her face. They were out of control.

The bus sped along, its engine rumbling monotonously. It bounced about in deep potholes, and my heart jolted in time with every road bump. Two or three hours later we reached our destination.

It was a hamlet in Sussex: a few tiny cottages, a church and church hall, a brooding place lost among the tall hedgerows. All around were farms, green fields, and narrow lanes overarched by trees. Unused to the countryside, lost, we were lined up at the roadside.

Where were the sandy beaches we'd been promised?

Chapter 2

The teachers marched us round to our billets. Mine was a cottage of sorts where I was to stay with Polly, whose father and brother worked on nearby farms. 'Polly's Cottage' I called it.

There was chaos during the days that followed. Some distressed children became so seriously disturbed that they had to be taken back home. But all my pleadings to be taken back home fell on deaf ears. Freddie ran away time and time again until he had to be taken home, for his own safety. Lucky Freddie! He was soon back home with Mum.

By day, Polly was a quiet, quaint woman, but at night she suffered from horrible nightmares. All the hair on my head stood up on its bristly ends on the first night in her cottage as I was woken by her screams. 'They're coming, they're coming!'

I took cover under my bed. I could hear her thrashing about in her delirium, the bedsprings groaning in sympathy. I reached up from my refuge, drew down blankets and pillows, and made myself a kind of air-raid shelter where I hid like a tortoise drawn back into its shell. I had a rough passage at birth and now I was facing another onslaught. I was a born jinx, born to suffer.

There were more disturbances the following night. On the next an almighty crash woke all of us: she had thrown her chamber pot out through the window. I got into my shelter in panic. Would she come after me? Who or what was after her?

Another night she tried to throw herself out of the window to see if she could fly. I rushed to find her father and brother and she fought them with a strength beyond what seemed possible in a woman. They finally managed to wake her out of the nightmare.

Sometimes she would march heavily up and down the stairs all night, worrying about those Germans who were coming to get her. So it became my nightly ritual to make my refuge under the bed. The first business of each morning was to set the bedclothes back tidily in their place so that nobody would suspect anything.

There was great excitement one morning when Polly could not be found. Eventually, to everyone's relief, she was found, in her nightdress, miles away. She had been sleepwalking. When the doctor questioned her, she had not the slightest recollection of what she had been doing.

During the day she was a delightful person, but her nightly behaviour got worse, until the strain on her family was such that I was transferred to a large farmhouse mansion at the opposite end of the village.

Our school stood across the lane from the church and church hall. It was an ancient rickety structure that appeared likely to collapse at any moment. Class 1 sat on a shaky stage, and faded curtains that had seen better days were drawn across so that lessons could be carried on out of sight of the other classes. These went on around the school heating system, a primitive pipe-stove. Lessons were quiet and orderly until one day, a teacher lighting the primus stove to boil a kettle, accidentally spilled the methylated spirit and dropped the match into it. Floating blue flames swept over the table, and soon everything was on fire. Amid wild shouts, we all tumbled outside.

Our dreams of a day off came to nothing, though. The fire was superficial and soon put out. Back we went to find that the great fire had only burned a few papers of no importance, and lessons resumed as if nothing had happened.

The school hut was a gloomy icebox, but there was nowhere else for us to go. From time to time warm drinks were handed round, but we suffered in comfortless surroundings with cold hands and chattering teeth. The isolated hamlet had no shop, no pub, no cafe, only rural solitude. All our needs had to be brought in from the large seaside town about half an hour's drive away.

There were things to enjoy, though. Our teachers produced a suitably patriotic play, 'Rule Britannia,' which played to a full house of local people. Our robust singing and dancing was almost too much for our weak stage. It shook and wobbled so much on its shaky foundations that we felt seasick, like the crew of a ship in a storm. Would it collapse, we wondered, and take us down with it? But we enjoyed the play so much we wished it could go on forever.

The only playground we had was in and around the church, but it was said to be haunted and we were told that there were vipers in the churchyard. This was guarded by massive iron gates and tall, dark fir trees resembling witches' hats.

During our play we would dare one another to do some very silly things. In those days neither churches nor church towers were kept locked, so the most daring of us would climb the spiral stairs to the top of the tower with loud, echoing shouts of scorn for the weaker brethren and then indulge in hijinks and jeers from the battlements. But our fear of ghosts remained, and an unexpected noise would send some of us scampering back down out of the church and across the yard to safety on the other side of the iron gates.

I was one of the less daring children, but eventually I and my friends managed to screw up our courage to attempt the spiral stair. 'If they can do it, so can I,' I assured myself as we crept up the lower steps. The higher we mounted, the more the walls pressed in to crush us, and as the stair narrowed the ghosts began to gather. Long before we reached the top our nerve broke and there was a mad, screeching, tangling rush back down, during which we tripped over each other's feet and ended in an untidy heap. We scrambled up and ran, our feet hardly touching the ground until we reached the road.

Sussex is an old, old county, and in the countryside beyond the hamlet the past came back to life. The woods and fields were said to be haunted by a fearsome ancient warrior clad in animal skins and brandishing in his powerful right hand a long, sharp spear. On my walkabouts I hoped to catch a glimpse of him and his retinue of screaming, ragged warrior women with their long flowing hair and wild ways.

Happily for me, though, I never caught so much as a glimpse of the wild huntsman or those wilder women who urged him on to lust or the shedding of blood.

Snakes were an important part of our childhood experience. One girl, playing alone by a hedge, saw one too late, panicked, turned to run away, and was bitten several times. We heard her screams and rushed to help, but when adults arrived they could find no puncture holes. She was taken back to the scene of the 'attack' and there, in the undergrowth, was a mottled twig. This twig, a clump of nearby stinging-nettles, and a vivid imagination accounted for her ordeal.

Later some naughty boys found a dead viper and pushed its head through a broken classroom window. The class, working quietly by themselves, broke into uproar, bringing their irate teacher quickly back. 'Sit down this instant!' she shouted.

'The snake, Miss, the snake,' we replied. But it had gone. 'Show me,' she shouted, 'Show me now.'

At once one of the boys drew it out from under his desk and held it out towards her, almost touching her face. Her legs gave way and she slumped to the floor in a dead faint, from which it took a long time for her concerned colleagues to revive her. Her first words on coming round were, 'Get rid of it. Get rid of it!'

Laughing loudly, the boys took it away and hid it for more fun later.

The prank worked well for us: we had easy lessons for the rest of that day and were sent home early. Next day the girls tried to get the boys to repeat the joke in the hopes of getting a whole day off and leaving the snake to take care of the empty classroom, but they refused, and I never did find out what happened to it.

When the nice people I was billeted with went away for a fortnight's holiday with their only daughter, they left me alone in the mansion with the housekeeper and cook, whom I very seldom saw. I was trusted to wander as I pleased and not to break anything.

At night, when the electricity was switched off for safety reasons, I had my own gilded candle holder. The candle's flickering flame made eerie leaping shadows as I crept down the dark corridor to the bathroom.

I spent my days in delighted exploration of this museum of a house. Its rooms were filled with antique furniture, pictures, treasures from the East, wonderfully carved wooden boxes and caskets that I was afraid to open, for fear of what might leap out and bite me.

One dark, claustrophobic corner resembled a beautiful mausoleum and contained a mysterious ancient lamp on a pedestal. One afternoon I dared to give it a few rubs, wait awhile, then a few more rubs. I ran quickly away, stopping at a distance in the hope that a genie would appear and grant me three wishes. What was that noise? The housekeeper? Was something following me? I did not wait to find out, but ran away as quickly and quietly as I could, vowing never again to touch anything valuable. I worshipped the riches around me and prayed that no falling bomb would destroy my magical museum.

Christmas arrived with old-fashioned hymn-singing in the packed church. It was a homely gathering of joyful people able, for that moment, to forget the war.

Winter was bleak, the high hedgerows drenched with cold rain, the dark lanes suitable only for the dead to walk in. When I went out, my echoing footsteps sounded like a follower at my heels, and in my fear I would break into a run.

We were warned time and again never to venture far from the hamlet and especially to keep out of the fields and the woods. Romney Marsh, nearby, was a dangerous area, a Prohibited Place where German parachutists might drop in and hide. We heard that a spy had been caught sending back secret radio messages. We longed to see a parachute floating to earth, but no such luck. Of course we ignored the warnings. Once we did get lost and had to be escorted home in an official military car — great fun, we thought.

Military activity began increasing on the roads: there were more vehicles, more uniforms. The war was noticeably creeping closer.

One day, in class, we were told to prepare ourselves for a further evacuation, this time to a far country called Wales. There was a mass protest and a riot of shouting: 'We want to go home!' We had only the vaguest notion about this distant place, where people lived in caves, wore animal skins, spoke an alien language, and disliked strangers. I longed to be at home where my heart was, with my Mum; we all did.

My happy sojourn at the mansion farmhouse came to an abrupt end. It was a sad farewell to all those kind-hearted people, every one of whom hugged and kissed me. From the lady of the house I received a supply of delicious egg sandwiches and instructions not to eat them all at once: 'You have a long and tedious journey ahead of you, my child. God bless you.'

So one Sunday morning in June 1940 our tram moved away and I was again the frightened girl upset by the uncertainty of it all. Herded against our will, we were like cattle bound for the slaughterhouse. 'Clunk-clunk-clunkity-clunk' went the speeding train over the rails, hammering out its monotonous message in words to hurt my heart: 'I want to go home, to go home to Mum. I want to go home, to go home....'

It was a waking nightmare of jerking movement, jolting points, a depressing stink of steam that caught my throat, and a sudden blast of gritty smoke when someone opened a window as we entered a tunnel. Children coughed and yelled as the smoke got into their eyes and throats. The boy who had opened the window was set upon by the rest of the boys and was in danger of being thrown out onto the track if the teachers had not taken him away for his own safety.

There were mysterious halts in unknown places, often on isolated sections of track. We listened to the sounds of guards' whistles and long wails, with no end in sight. A careful watch had to be kept in case a bored child would jump out and try to run home.

Some of us were able to sleep, but many wept in sheer frustration. The most active among us played tag about the corridors and got into mischief. I lost count of the number of diversions we took to avoid the bombers, but we were on the move for more than fourteen hours.

At last the train began to move more slowly, its stops became more prolonged, and finally, on a Sunday evening, it ground to a stop. Where we were was beyond anyone's wildest guess.

Looking out, we saw a lively port and had dreams of a long sea voyage. A ship was there, as well as a lot of station personnel and many servicemen and women in uniform. Each separate group had its own urgencies. The military personnel stood to one side, distinguished by the huge clouds of cigarette smoke that rose above their heads. Impatient porters struggled with laden trollies, unmindful of those they knocked into.

Tired and stiff-legged, we were drawn up in lines on a clear section of platform to be checked and counted. That over, we were allowed to move about, stretch our sore limbs and get our circulation going. A fresh breeze off the sea flapped our identity labels up against our chins as we ran about in play.

In the distance an assortment of buses and other vehicles awaited us. The order was given, so we picked up our belongings, marched out, and were helped into our seats.

We moved away in convoy — to the caves in the mountains, I wondered? In each town's narrow, twisting streets the bus had to slow almost to a stop to negotiate turns. Then we were in the country again among an abundance of wildflowers, tree-lined hedgerows, and fields where wild rabbits moved about in happy play, oblivious to the crows and seagulls screeching overhead.

We passed through village after village until finally we reached one closed in, it seemed, by a range of mountains. We stopped outside its wide-fronted village-hall.

We disembarked and went into the building to sit on forms ranged along the walls. Kind women brought us glasses of milk and Marie biscuits to refresh us as we waited for arrangements to be made for our dispersal. Then our names were called out and we got up to meet our 'aunties,' who spoke a language we could not understand, but they were kindly and compassionate. How many aunties can one have? I wondered. How many uncles? Name after name was called, 'auntie' after 'auntie' collected her 'nieces' or 'nephews.'

'Beryl Mills,' the voice said, and in my ears alarm bells began to ring.

Chapter 3

Two stone-faced women confronted me, unsmiling, without a friendly word. I recoiled, rigid with fear, my mind dark with nameless premonition. I refused to go with them and made a violent scene. The other people and my fellow evacuees stared at me in amazement. 'Leave me alone!' I yelled. 'I don't want to go anywhere with you. Leave me alone!'

Even the two women were astonished at my hostility. I could see the spite in their dark eyes and their faces turning red with rage at finding their authority flouted. I anchored myself against the wall, clinging to the form as they seized my arms and tried to drag me along with them. The pain was excruciating, but I was not going to let go even if they broke my arm.

Suddenly I lost my anchorage and the three of us crashed down together on the floor, giving a striking display of their dark blue drawers. Children watched wide-eyed and the local people expressed loud astonishment at the behaviour of their distinguished neighbours.

Some of the boys tried to drag me away, shouting at my captors to let me go and getting in a few well-aimed kicks, but it was no good. The two relentless old women held my arms and head in their vice-like grip, pulling back on my hair until I could hardly breathe.

'Heavens above!' they cried. 'Don't be such a silly girl. Come along quietly, you'll see your friends tomorrow. Stop your nonsense for goodness sake. We'll be the talk of the village.'

They were too strong for me in the end and dragged me away. I was still trying my utmost to break free, shouting at the top of my voice to all and sundry. 'Let me go! Go and find another girl. I hate you, you're hurting me. Please help, somebody.'

But the villagers were afraid of these two holier-than-thou sisters. I was under arrest, frog-marched through the village with people tut-tutting and shaking their heads to see a little girl so brutally handled.

At last I was half dragged, half carried to a large, depressing house with a narrow lane and parking space in front of it. They had my head held down so low that I couldn't see where I was going. The next thing I knew I had been thrown like a disobedient dog into a tiny, dark room and the door locked behind me. I looked round for some means of escape, but there was none.

We had heard that Welsh people lived in dark caves. This was one of them. What awful danger would I have to face next?

Thinking, I suppose, that a few hours in solitary might moderate my temper, they left me alone for what seemed a very long time. Then the door was opened and in came a cheerful maid with tea and cakes so tiny I might have been Alice in Wonderland. She told me that I was in the vicarage, that she was Gwen, the maid, and that she worked for the bachelor vicar, Reverend Guto James, and his three spinster sisters: Miss Elen, Miss Beti, and Miss Eva.

I learned that in this house there was a strictly disciplined daily routine that nothing was allowed to interfere with. Gwen was required to change her uniform twice a day, once for the morning and once for the afternoon. The stone-faces had instructed her to make it clear that my role was to be, as far as possible, neither seen nor heard. I was not to involve myself in any way in the daily life of the vicarage. This tiny kitchen and my bedroom were to be my world.

I sat in my chair. Gwen floated in and out like a ghost, getting on with her work in silence. Then the door flew open as if kicked, a hand placed a small glass of milk of the table, a voice spoke the one word, 'Drink!' and the door closed again. One gulp and the milk was gone.

A head appeared round the door, a finger beckoned and a shadow led the way up to the attic bedroom, where I was expected to undress quickly, leap into bed, and drop into a disciplined coma. The door was slammed shut with a clap of noise that echoed through the entire silent house. There I stood, shaking like a leaf in a storm.

Pushed into a cold, strange bedroom, alone for the first time in my young life, I stared out at the western sky and resolved by hook or by crook to run away the first chance I got.

The door crashed open again, making me jump. Standing in the doorway, with the light behind her, was a formidable woman with a man's voice, harsh and without feeling. Why wasn't I in bed as I'd been told? Her barked words were a physical hurt to me; I'd never been spoken to like this in my whole life. She marched across to the bed, shook it until it rattled the floorboards and said, 'Get in now, at once, little girl.'

I slipped out of my clothes and into bed as the door crashed shut behind her, raising clouds of dust. Then she was gone, the living-dead, the black witch, back into the darkness.

The overpowering stillness frightened me even more than the noise. I wasn't a bit tired, so with an aching heart I got up and looked out of the window. I longed to fly away back over those mountains to the mother I needed so much. I saw a distant light sparkling over the dark sea and thought of home. 'Mum, where are you? I'm thinking of you, I need you. I'm so alone. Please come for me.'

The bedroom door slammed open again, its explosive noise shattering the unholy silence. My heart gave a great jump. Everything went black. The next thing I knew, there was a sharp pain in my side where a pointed shoe was pushing against my ribs. 'Rise and return to bed!' said the commanding voice. 'I hope I'm not going to have to tell you again. Obey and get into that bed, you.'

Too weak to stand, I crawled on hands and knees back to bed. I've no idea how I managed to get into it, but as soon as I did I pulled the bedclothes up over my head. An earthquake threw me from side to side. That creepy old crow was standing over me. I could hear her harsh breathing as she shook the bed in her vile temper. The earthquake died away; heavy footsteps echoed out of the room. I tried to relax.

They were playing a game with me. I could hear the floorboards creak as she listened outside the door, waiting for a chance to catch me out of bed. From time to time the door was opened a crack to check on me. I did my best to suppress my terrified thoughts and tried to pace my heart into a slower rhythm.

In the twilight I dozed off, only to wake at the sound of screaming and find that all was quiet. Surely I must have awakened the whole house. I slept again and was again shaken by invisible hands and woke again, heart pounding, waiting for something dreadful to happen.

Night after night I was left alone in that bedroom with my fear, knowing that callous eyes secretly watched me, hands waited to pounce on any wrong move, and voices saved up their venom to assault me.

I suffered nightmares. One that recurred had me jumping on and off the bed, screaming incessantly . . . were they sticking needles into a waxen image? I saw myself tortured, felt a huge arm reach out at me, and passed out. Surely I was dead, but it was light, it was morning, and Gwen was calling me to get up and go to school.

My sleep was so often disturbed by the terrors of the night that in the mornings I woke with a sick headache and had to drag myself into my clothes. Out on my feet, I had no appetite for breakfast, and those women did not seem to care if I lived or starved to death.

I went to school with my fellow evacuees. We had lessons on National Security. If a stranger were to ask us about the village or the district, we must remain silent. On no account must we tell that person anything, for walls had ears. I knew the vicarage walls did. There, on the walls of our playground, large ears were chalked.

Although I did not feel at all well, it was some relief to be among friends. Those who were billeted near the school would go home for the midday meal; those living too far away brought their own sandwiches and pop. I was expected to return to the vicarage for my midday meal, but I was so afraid of the place that I would only pretend to go and instead walk about with my friends, who were always ready to share their sandwiches. My drink was water from the stream nearby.

At first we evacuees were regarded with suspicion as well as curiosity. Soon, however, the kind villagers put their suspicions aside and accepted us as 'plant y sais,' or 'children of the English.' Various reasons led to some among us returning or being sent home, but I never had that luck.

Being full of natural curiosity and an appetite for adventure, I should not have minded if my billet had been a kindly one. But my regime was very strict. I must be dumb, subdued, reserved, always seen but not heard. Eternal silence forced me into patient readings and re-readings of 'Alice in Wonderland,' but I challenged Carroll's whimsical nonsense: the three sisters were as grotesque as any character of his. I knew them for real, and my experience was of real life and not funny at all.

You'd have thought those three spinsters would have had something better to do than watch me all the time, without ever a kind word — only criticism if ever I stepped outside their straight and narrow lines. I soon realised that it did not matter much what I did. I was always in the wrong just by being there.

Our religious knowledge lessons taught us that hell was down below, in the bowels of the earth, but I knew it wasn't — it was in that vicarage, and those three stone-faced women were the devil's disciples. My bedroom door was the entrance to the worst part of hell, guarded by the foul presence of the demon-sisters under the direction of the oldest one.

I had to go home at the end of school, and then I got a small cup of tea, a slice of bread and butter cut in two, and half a teaspoonful of jam. The meal was timed to the second, and being late meant cold tea; to ask for a second cup was a cardinal sin. I was sent off to bed by 7:30 and would lie there for hours, pretending to sleep.

Every so often the three witches would creep in on tiptoe and I would watch them through slitted eyes as they gathered around me, whispering. What did they want? Once, one of them pushed her face too close to mine. I smelled her foul breath and spat in her face, causing her to spring back as if kicked by a donkey. Her hand was raised to strike, but one of her sisters whispered. 'She's having one of her nightmares,' and away they floated.

I was never allowed to bring my friends to the vicarage to play, and when visitors were expected I had to be got rid of. I heard one of the sisters say that I must not be let near because I was not family, and Gwen would be sent to tell me to go and play somewhere and not return until late.

I could be happy then: we children did not really understand that a terrible war was going on. We were protected from its horrors by the beautiful, wild, and wonderful hilly countryside through which we could wander, over hill and dale and by narrow twisting roads to the winding river, the sandy beaches and the lovely expansive deep blue sea.

Three of us used to go walking and playing the fool, but we were warned to stay away from a smallholding known as the Garden of Eden. There lived a vindictive, Bible-carrying farmer, 'Iesu Bach,' who owned a fine orchard hill of delicious apples 'Beware!' we were told, 'Don't you never go near that place.'

We did, of course, and there were trees loaded with ripe apples set among lawn-like grass nibbled short by sheep. Nobody was around, the apples were inviting, could we manage one each — and perhaps one more?

Quiet as mice we crept on all fours through the hedge, reached the trees, and each picked an apple. No sooner had we done so than we were rounded up by vicious sheepdogs snapping their sharp teeth. If they were wild, their master was wilder, a giant in a violent temper. The very trees seemed to shake in fear of him as he rushed towards us, crook in hand. 'The Lord hath found thee out, heathen children,' he bellowed, poking his crook at us. 'Thou shall not steal. Hold them there, dogs.'

He went away and returned carrying a massive Bible. 'Now,' he said, 'Put one hand on the tree and the other on this Bible. Look not at me. Look at the tree and repeat after me: "Sorry for stealing your babies."' This we did. 'Now kiss this Holy Bible, and the apple tree, and line up on your knees before me.' He placed on the head of each one of us the apple she had scrumped. We held ourselves very still, afraid to let it fall off. Then he opened his Bible and in a deep, sonorous voice read out a number of extracts in Welsh. 'O Iesu Mawr, let me know thy will,' he groaned. 'What punishment shall I visit upon these thieving sinners?'

It was too much. He was so comical that we could not control ourselves and we laughed and laughed. The apples fell to the ground—the last straw. He lost control of himself.

'Stand up, sinners!' he roared. 'The Judgement is at hand.' There was no possibility of making a run for it—the dogs watched our every move.

'Turn and face the trees of God!' shouted Iesu Bach. When we had done so, we felt sharp stinging pains on the backs of our bare legs. We were not laughing now. He was whipping us with stinging nettles. We danced in pain and cried out louder and louder as he kept on switching us.

At last he stopped, saying, 'Take that as the punishment of the Lord, and away with you through the front gate.' We ran faster than we had ever run in our lives. Only when we had put some distance between us did we stop to comfort ourselves with dock leaves. Somewhere between tears and laughter we vowed never to go near that place again. 'Silly Bible fool,' we giggled. 'Damn! Those nettles did pinch.'

On other occasions we would see Iesu Bach standing beside a boulder over which he had draped a red cloth. This was his altar, and on either side of him sat an acolyte sheepdog attentive to his preaching. From a safe distance we threw crab apples, but they fell short. There were a few religious maniacs roaming the Blessed Hills, and Iesu was a great character, a walking Bible who bore no ill-will to any, save those who dared trespass in his Garden of Eden.

Chapter 4

With war raging in the outside world, one would not have thought that hymn-singing could cause offence to anyone. It could, however, if it took place in the public house. Then the Chapel establishment took strong objection, and any young man they saw singing there would be named and shamed.

The Chapel Deacon's son, home on convalescent leave after being wounded in action, became one of the victims of these holier-than-thou's.

Complaints were made to his parents, and they instructed him to conform while at home in the village, and on no account to sing hymns in the pub again. He took offence, got his kit and returned to his regiment without a word to his father and mother.

Later he was killed in action and a feud broke out. Believing that had he not returned prematurely he would not have been killed, his distraught parents broke with the Chapel, burned their Bibles on the Chapel steps and came to blows with the elders. 'You killed my son, you unholy crowd of hypocrites,' said the father, and he threatened to burn down the Chapel with its congregation inside.

He, his wife, and the rest of their family never attended religious worship again for the rest of their lives. It was a pity that only the loss of loved ones in battle could make people take the war seriously and realise that no amount of hymn-singing and daft sermonising could bring the dead back to life.

Meanwhile, I continued to endure the nightmare of life at the vicarage, my every move watched by the three dark sisters. Miss Elen was the oldest, tall, broad-shouldered, black hair, and penetrating eyes darker than coal. She had been a V.A.D. [Voluntary Aid Detachment, or a volunteer nursing assistant] in the First World War, but there was not an atom of compassion in her: she appeared to have neither feelings nor sympathy for any living thing.

Miss Eva, short and plump, resembled a chicken as much as anything. She had fair hair and brown eyes and was the family's cook.

Miss Beti, built like an athlete, had mousy hair and eyes that were grey or green depending on how the light caught them. Her speciality was make-do-and-mend, and she acted as general dogsbody to her sisters.

The Reverend Guto James, tall, sparely built, and white-haired, was always well-groomed and dressed immaculately, as befitted one in high authority. He had ice-blue eyes and mice in his shoes—they squeaked as he walked. Their home seemed to me to be surrounded by a barrier of evil which excluded all wildlife: there was never a bird or animal to be seen in the grounds, and the golden rule of dead silence prevailed.

One day I returned to the vicarage to find that a letter had arrived from my mother asking if she could visit for a few days. I was on a cloud nine of happiness in anticipation, but I was not allowed to remain very long up there.

'Out of the question!' they told me. 'We have no room for her.' Nor would they make any effort to find her accommodation in the village. Happiness and life itself drained away. I knew there was room—they had guests at times. I felt that I would never see Mum again.

The way to my bedroom was barred by some evil presence at the foot of the stairs. I gathered my courage and leapt through it up the first three steps. Half-way up I had to rest, weak-kneed and trembling in the darkness. I closed the bedroom door and was alone with my desolation, longing to see Mum, put my arms around her, hold her, hear her comforting voice and have news of home. I seemed to see her stretching out her arms and calling, but I was not able to reach her. How could they deny me my mother?

Where were their Christian values, their alleged belief in a merciful god? And how my hurt was doubled and redoubled when friends left to go home.

The three ghouls degraded me spiritually and I had no defence against the process. They must have been aware of my anxieties but never reported them to the authorities. They must have known of my profound unhappiness, but like the dog in the manger, they would not let me go elsewhere.

Then one of the evacuee girls died and the body was taken home to be buried. The tragedy was with us for weeks.

Christmas came and we went from door to door carol singing, but not to the vicarage: nobody dared sing there. If we sang in English, we might get a penny, or nothing at all. If we sang in English and Welsh, we got up to tuppence. But when we sang all the way through in Welsh, sixpence. When the evening was over I had six shillings. I was the wealthiest girl in the world.

Next morning I slipped out to the village shop and bought some beautiful patterned handkerchiefs as a Christmas present for Mum. When I explained what I wanted them for, the sympathetic shopkeeper exchanged them for some of better quality from her stock, parcelled them up and made sure I had enough money left to pay the postage. So touched was she to see how I had used my carol money that she gave me a big bag of delicious toffees.

I thanked her with tears in my eyes and ran all the way to the post office, elated with the knowledge that there were still lovely people in the world. The day was dark and cloudy, but a bright sun shone in my heart.

When I got back to the vicarage, Gwen had left her bicycle leaning against the garage doors. Thinking myself unobserved, and seeing no harm in it, I took a ride to the entrance gates and back. The three sisters were waiting, and the expression on their faces suggested I had committed a serious crime.

'Leave things alone that don't belong to you!' one of them shouted, while another shook me off the bike, kicked me, and shouted, 'Take it back at once, you little thief!' She aimed a blow at my head, but I managed to avoid it.

Not willing to be outdone, the third sister seized me by the shoulders and shook me, screaming into my face, 'Do as you're told, you little sneak, or I'll tear you into pieces. Get moving this instant.' I could see all the way down her big black throat.

I rushed to put the bicycle back where it belonged, but it slipped, knocked against a ladder, and brought down a coil of rope and a can of paint. I left everything in a mess and made a run for it. I wasn't going to let them catch me anywhere near that rope. They were in the mood for a lynching party. Handfuls of thrown gravel chipped at my heels as I fled.

Once my friends went to the beach, but the sisters wouldn't let me go. When I got home from school the following day, I found a cardboard box full of sand. My friends had brought the beach to me!

One day I decided to play tennis against the vicarage wall. What I did not know was that the Holy Man was on the other side of it, preparing his Sunday sermon. 'Thump, thump, thump,' went the ball and suddenly out came Miss Eva with her long-handled floor-brush. Was she going to fly? Brush raised, she came at me, but I kept my distance.

'You troublesome bitch!' she screamed. 'Distracting the vicar in his study! Disturbing his sacred concentration! Go elsewhere and play quietly if you know what's good for your health!'

I ran off to play ball against the garage and out leapt another outraged harridan, yelling, 'How dare you knock the ball against those noisy doors!'

Snatching the racket from my hand, she hit me over the head with it and flung it over the garden wall, then tossed the ball after it. I high-tailed it out of her sight.

One Saturday morning I was out walking with friends. The lanes were ablaze with colour, and we saw a snake in the middle of the road. Shocked with a nameless fear, we started running back the way we had come when up rode a tiny postman on a miniature Post Office bicycle. Seeing that we were afraid, he leapt off his bike, picked up the snake, and put it into his mailbag. We thought that he was preparing to throw the snake at us, so we ran for the field gate and scrambled over it.

But he only laughed at our silliness. He took the reptile out of his bag, and laid it gently in the grass between us and the gate. He had put the snake there for its own safety, but we thought that it would come after us, and we ran in a wild panic round the hedgerows looking for a way out. Eventually we found a gap wide enough to crawl through and regain the road and safety.

It was all very well for people to say that there was nothing whatever to be afraid of in a harmless grass snake, but how were we evacuees to know that? We were instinctively afraid of all snakes.

The snake haunted my dreams that night and I slept very little. Next morning I made my bed neatly, washed and dressed and made my way to the kitchen for breakfast. That day it was damp, limp, water-fried bread which I could not face, so I wrapped it in my handkerchief and threw it over the garden wall as soon as I got outside. If the birds didn't want it, the slugs and snails would.

Unfortunately the soggy mess was discovered by the gardener-handyman, a Chapel deacon who walked with a limp said to have been caused by catching his foot in a rabbit-trap. Famous for snitching, this two-faced sneak took enormous pleasure in causing trouble, especially for me. He showed the disgusting remains of my breakfast to the three ghouls. They ground their teeth with rage and could not wait for me to get home from school.

'Don't you know there's a war on?' they shouted. 'How dare you waste good food!'

'You know I hate fried bread,' I replied. 'You never eat it, so why make me?'

I had to apologize to each of them in turn, and to the dog I said, 'What's the matter with your fried bread?' To them I said, 'The dog won't eat it, nor the birds, nor even the slugs and snails. Was it the dog's pee you fried it in?'

A fiery cloud of angry babble echoed around the kitchen. The dog joined in, barking loudly. They could none of them stand backchat from a brainless evacuee. The wily gardener, delighted at the storm he had raised, slunk quietly away, and I went off to find better company in the village, ignoring the shouts of 'Come back here at once, you ungrateful child!'

When I got to the bridge, I laid my face against the rough stones and wept bitterly. There I was taken pity on by a kind-hearted woman who lived nearby. 'Come in and have a cup of tea, *cariad*,' she said.

She had two daughters of her own and an evacuee girl living with her. I was made heartily welcome and told them everything. She knew perfectly well how I was being treated; the whole village knew, of course, but what could they do against the power and status of the vicarage?

'Nobody will change places with you, you know that, don't you?' she said. 'All the evacuees know about those three horrible sisters. We all do. They pretend to be holy and upright, but they're vindictive she-devils underneath. They daren't walk in the village until the children are all at school because the children would follow them around and annoy them.'

Gwen had been sent to find me, but after vainly searching for some time she had given up. Later I climbed the garden wall, sneaked along under the bushes, and managed to get unobserved across the yard. I climbed onto the outhouse and from there I was able to reach the landing window. I crept to my bedroom, quietly shut the door and jammed a chair under the handle.

I was wakened later by the sound of somebody trying to get in, but I had done my job too well for them. Short of breaking the chair, there was no way to get in. After a while she, or they, went away and left me in peace for the rest of the night.

I got such a telling-off at breakfast, though, that I left the food uneaten on the table and rushed out into the clean air to walk to school. From the hedges I picked edible plants and put them in my pockets to see me through the day. If they were going to treat me like an animal, I might as well eat like one, I thought.

For the next few weeks they maintained a conspiracy of silence against me. They withdrew. I saw only the occasional shadow from one day to the next.

Gwen was given notice to keep out of my sight, too. I might have been living alone in that awful dark house.

Luckily I made friends with a lovely Welsh schoolgirl who invited me to her home. I followed her along the mountain road for what seemed a very long time, but it did not matter as it was Saturday morning. The land around was steep, but it levelled out into areas where sheep liked to graze. The farm nestled in a sheltered corner, out of the winds and winter weather. As we drew near, I could hear the happy voices of children at play. My heart sank as I wondered what kind of welcome I was going to get.

But my new friend's extravert Mam was a tonic for me, a breath of pure, clean mountain air. Nothing ever dismayed her. She ruled her children with a very light rod indeed, and her home was quite free of the bitterness and tensions I had been enduring. Inside, the house was a comfortable jumble of furniture and farm implements among which happy-faced children of various ages ran free, having the time of their lives.

Never had I seen such a generous and abundant display of food as was on her table, all baked and cooked by her. Table manners did not matter here, nor was there grace before meals, just a boisterous freedom to eat what one liked in whatever manner one wished. It was like a dream come true, and tears welled up in my eyes and ran down my cheeks. This was Alice in Wonderland country: children allowed to grow up in their own way with the support of an affectionate mother who never scolded, nagged, or regimented them.

This most delightful of mothers remained patient among the clattering activity. If the children got really out of hand, though, she would call in their father, who had a quick temper and a loud voice and would stand no nonsense from any of them. He would catch them up, shake them gently and, with a sharp tap on the bottom, still their clamour. 'Don't you dare annoy your Mam,' he would say. He would not have dreamed of hurting them physically, and his gruff manner was mainly bluff, but they knew they must do as they were told—for a while, at least.

I understood hardly a word of the rapid chatter that passed between parents and children because it was all in Welsh. I was a stranger in their midst, but my school friend helped me follow what was going on as we sat opposite one another on a long, rough form.

The senior sheepdog, a fine-looking animal, had his own place at table and sat there watching closely as we ate, ever-ready to snap up the morsels of food that were thrown to him. If he was ignored, he would give a comical look and a half-howl, half-bark until another morsel came his way. He was so spoilt that he refused to eat from his bowl on the floor. He was no common dog but one of the family.

The food was plain and plentiful: a great chunk of lean meat, steaming bowls of potatoes and vegetables, lashings of brown gravy rich in meat-juice. Then we had apple pie and custard. The meal took us a good hour of relaxed eating and chatter and nobody took any more notice of me than of any other member of the family. When this family's children brought friends home they were treated as family members.

The father ate at a separate table, with his back to the fire. After a while, he looked at me and said, 'Is it true, then, what they say about these people you're living with, that they boil their kippers?'

'Now then, Dai,' said his wife. 'Don't bother the girl.'

'People do say,' he went on, 'that they boil their kippers until they're soft, then they eat the flesh and save the backbone and play fish-music on it with a needle.'

'I don't know,' I said. 'They don't let me see what they get up to. I'm only allowed into two rooms, the scullery and my bedroom. I don't often see anybody, they keep me separate.'

'Duw annwyl!' he burst out. 'Holy devils. That's no way to treat a child.'

'Keep calm, now, Dai,' his wife said. 'Don't be getting excited.'

We went out to play and for me to have a good look round. Sacks were used for shawls on the farm, held in place by wooden pins. Aprons and leggings were worn for protection against thorns and cold weather. The kitchen was a kind of museum, with all kinds of implements hung round the walls on long nails. The rafters were loaded with tools of various kinds — there were even implements inside the wide chimney. Nothing was thrown away here in case it came in useful in the future.

This farming family knew that the war was going on. They saw and heard the aeroplanes that flew over them. But there was nothing that they could do about it except carry on farming, so why worry? Live for the day and let tomorrow take care of itself. They existed almost in isolation and possessed something no money can buy: integration, inner harmony, carefree happiness.

The wild life around that farm was part of the pattern, in no danger from that family; there was not a gun in the place. They made me feel completely at home and did a great deal to heal my wounds. Their way of life, so natural and secure, would not last very much longer, God bless them.

Chapter 5

How do I know what I think till I hear what I say? – Alice.

I shall keep a diary and keep it very secret. It will come in very handy one day in the distant future to show to Mum, who will lovingly read every word and be pleased, but mainly shocked, by my experiences.

Only once more did I go walking the upland trails with my farm friend, taking shortcuts over the moorland. At our secret rendezvous, where the hardcore road came into view below, we said our farewells. I had always known that these escapes were far too good to last; tears used to run down my face at every parting. Her gentle eyes sparkled with friendship. She was the only true pal I had to share my troubles with.

I ran down fast as a deer, leaping over the scattered boulders. When I stopped for breath I could see her away up the hill, a distant hand waved and she was gone.

The tell-tale gardener had found out where I was going and passed on the information to the three ghoul sisters, and I was forbidden to go up the mountain again. I had had wonderful chats with my friend, and it was heart-breaking to explain, when I saw her at school next day, that I had made my last visit to the farm. I told her how the evil gardener spied on me, how my life was one of solitude, how they were killing me with their silence and kept me in after school. How all I had to eat when I got back from school was half a glass of buttermilk and a slice of bread with a scraping of butter.

One time I decided I would prefer to take my refreshment in my own room. It was a mistake, for scarcely had I set foot in the passage when there was a sudden shout. 'Get back! Get back at once. No food is to be taken upstairs. Get back into the scullery where you belong. Who do you think you are, my goodness!'

How could she have known? Could they hear my breathing?

Every time I climbed the stairs I studied each step carefully to see if there was some hole through which I was being spied on and reported. Did the mice spy for the three sisters, reporting my every movement? Was there some kind of instant telepathic connection?

I must have dozed off. I was in a twilight-zone, mouth a-gape, eyes staring, full of tears, at some panic vision. Mum, her arms outstretched, reaching out for me, appealing, pleading. What could she want? Was this a premonition?

I leaped out of bed, landing on the floorboards with a thump, crying out, 'Mum, what's wrong?' Light reflected on the window panes. I looked out. Was she there still? My mind was screaming, 'Mum, come back to me!'

She wasn't there. I hammered my fists on the panes until my wrists were numb. What did this nightmare mean? Why was she reaching out to me? Was there to be no end to the vortex of night-horrors? I did not return to bed but lay on the bare floorboards under the window all night long, untroubled by the discomfort, and tottered off to school next morning without breakfast, nibbling again at whatever edibles I could find along the hedgerows.

The Holy Man held a special service, one Wednesday, for us evacuees. He was wasting everybody's time, his own included. Nobody took any notice of his foolish rantings. Whose side was his god on? If God was our help, why didn't he end the war so that we could all go home?

His god wasn't much help to the vicar either; he went down that winter with a variety of illnesses including a nasty, rasping chesty cough. He was so ill that another clergyman had to stand in for him, and even at the worst point in his illness he did not stop smoking heavily. But he did take his doctor's excellent advice to keep away from cigarettes. He bought the longest cigarette-holder he could find. And he went on, like Alice's caterpillar, puffing and puffing.

Deprived of my visits to the farm, I studied the three vicarage devils. I saw that they wore clothes that had been fashionable in the 1920s and that their code of conduct was Victorian. They did not call each other by their Christian names but rather 'Miss Elen' or 'Miss Beti' or 'Miss Eva.'

Miss Elen was Big Boss, military in bearing, her figure manly and clad, in winter in a brown trench coat that reached her ankles. A bulky fox-fur wrapped her neck and fell over her shoulders. She looked like a palm tree with legs, and I was always hoping that the fox would bury his sharp teeth in her jugular vein. On her head was an expensive wide-brimmed hat that kept her features in shadow, and she wore expensive long black gloves and galoshes over her shoes.

Miss Beti had a long, light-brown fur coat and large fur hat to match. The locals called her 'Cat-Woman,' which suited her spiteful nature. She had soft brown shoes, with galoshes and bulky fur gloves.

Miss Eva, the weakest minded of the three, wore a long camel hair coat and a hat so large as to resemble an Australian bushman's. She was an oddball of a woman, with a one-track mind. She wore heavy shoes and mittens like boxing gloves. She invariably did precisely as her sisters told her and carried out their orders with strict efficiency.

One time I fell ill and was confined to bed, and although a doctor lived next door, they never asked him to visit me. They treated me like an animal; perhaps if I stopped breathing they'd call the vet? Miss Elen, who fancied herself a medic, looked into my bedroom, then walked away, saying, 'She'll get over it.' The truth is, she was afraid that whatever I had might be contagious and she dared not enter my room. She ordered her sisters to stay well clear and to make sure the window was kept wide open.

It was Gwen who had to see to me, but all she did was bring me something to eat and drink. If I needed more water, I was to use what was left in my hot water bottle, and that had gone ice cold. I was shivering so much that the bed danced on its slender legs. I was a wartime Cinderella with no hope of a Prince Charming to come to my rescue—out of sight, out of mind. The only thing that kept me sane was my books, 'Alice in Wonderland' especially, and 'Alice Through the Looking-Glass.' I felt that I had much in common with Alice in the looking-glass world of the vicarage.

When important visitors came, I had to be paraded in front of them in a borrowed dress to demonstrate the family's commitment to the war effort. I must make myself presentable for the occasion, be spick and span, and be seen but not heard. I was under strict orders to use my mouth for eating only. I would sit stiff as a dummy, head held high, shoulders back, my every move slow and mechanical. 'Never take your mouth to your food. Use your fingers to carry it to your face. Take a small bite, then convey the rest back to your plate. Chew your food carefully and slowly, be elegant. If you embarrass us you'll live to regret it.'

The sandwiches were paper-thin, as was the bread and butter—I could see the plate's pattern through them. I sat there grimly wishing that I had Alice and the White Rabbit to talk to, bored stiff with the sisters' toffee-nosed acting and slick palaver.

Watching me were the Cheshire Cat, the Mad Hatter, the Walrus, and the Carpenter. This was how I saw the visitors as they sat there, eating so elegantly, chewing endlessly and occasionally falling into periods of stiff silence. I was starving — I could have eaten my plate in the desperation of my hunger. Eventually I had an urgent need for the lavatory. I fidgeted and shifted my bottom. If looks could have killed, I'd have been struck dead.

At last the long-drawn-out session was coming to an end. Visitors stood about in groups, gossiping. I might have been invisible; nobody said a word to me. Then they started up again with dreary words of thanks too many times repeated. I was chewing my spit, and my stomach twisted with hunger. My brain was urging me to spread blackberry jam on the Bible and devour it.

Finally they dragged themselves away and I could disappear back to the kitchen and change out of my pretty dress. Gwen gave me a generous thick crust of bread with plenty of jam on it and I took it and ran as fast as I could to the ty bach [toilet], where I chewed and peed simultaneously. Glorious the relief to my bursting bladder and empty stomach, and to hell with stupid conventions.

In my ice-cold bedroom I shivered under the sheet, a single blanket, and the showpiece bedspread. The earthenware hot water bottle held no warmth; its true purpose was to provide water for me to wash myself in the morning. After washing, I would take my bowl down to the scullery, scour it, and return it to its stand. I would then take down my chamber pot if I had used it during the night, re-fill the hot water bottle, and return both to the bedroom. This was the daily routine, and everything must be clean and in its place for the daily inspection. If anything was out of place I got an unholy row.

I was allowed to use the indoor bathroom only on Friday evenings for my weekly bath, a quick dip-and-dry, then out. The bath must be cleaned until it sparkled and I must never use the W.C.

The school holidays came and I enjoyed a rare and sandy treat with my classmates, a trip to the beach. We swam, then dressed and lay on the sand, the hot sun burning our backs. But one girl, more daring than the rest of us, swam out too far and was carried away on the currents. We shouted and screamed for help, in panic as we saw her go under, arms waving frantically. She was a goner.

But no, the mountain gods must have heard our prayers. A fishing boat was on the scene and the men pulled her aboard and saved her life. She recovered but later suffered bad headaches. Her distraught parents came and took her back home. So uncertain was the life of the evacuee—at one moment best friends, the next isolated again.

Solitary in my kitchen cell, Alice in Evacueeland, I surrounded myself with my book friends. Things grew curiouser and curiouser. 'Dear me, how queer everything is today. Yesterday everything was as usual. I wonder if I've been changed in the night? I get awfully confused by my nightmares.'

'Was I myself when I got up this morning? I almost think I can remember feeling different....Who in the vicarage am I? Oh, dear, what nonsense I'm talking.'

Two thin slices of bread on the table were labelled 'Eat me.' The half-glass of buttermilk shouted, 'Drink me.' Was I going mad, after all? I should have to go back to the horrid nightmares of that poky bedroom, with no toys to play with, so many hateful lessons to learn. Who was I, then, what was I? I burst into tears like Alice. How weary I was of being here all alone.

Sometimes selected people were invited to the vicarage for Prayers, such bores, all sillies, acting sillier, the mournful vicar so slow in his deliberations, the solemn divine messages. His voice dwindled until only the deaf or the church mice could hear. The whole situation was absurd to Alice, but the characters looked so grave that she could not laugh. I bent my head still lower, made myself look solemn, my toes meanwhile wriggling as if there were mice in my shoes.

Miss Eva was not quite right in the head. During holidays I had been told to dust the stairs down every Friday morning, but the first time I did so she flew into a rage. 'Get away from those stairs,' she shouted. 'That's my housework, worm!'

'Miss Elen ordered me to dust them down.'

'It's my work, do you hear, mine. Get out of my sight you silly little worm.'

I could see her thinking, 'Off with her head! Send for the Executioner. Here comes a chopper to chop off her head.'

She had a vicious temper and, not wanting a clout across the face, I ran to the open front door to escape. The dog raced out with me, and I called back, 'Miss Eva, your dog has run out.'

'Don't you dare call him dog, his name is Mr Tom and don't you forget it. Mr Tom.' She fetched her broom, and I drew farther off, not willing to risk my luck. She got Mr Tom indoors and, before closing the door, told me, 'Mr Tom is one of the family and you are not. You are only a temporary resident and you had better keep well out of my sight, you miserable worm.'

I went away and played. On returning, I was confronted by not one but three Red Queens demanding why I had not cleaned the stairs. I had no excuse, and Miss Eva said not a word m my defence. My punishment was to be shut in my bedroom again. No point in arguing.

Later, in the kitchen, I noticed an open tin of dried milk. Curious, I dipped in my finger and licked it. The taste reminded me of sherbet. Miss Eva, the cook, had not noticed, so quickly I poured a little into the palm of my hand and licked it. Then she saw me, looked in the tin and asked, 'Have you been at this powder?' In all innocence, 'Yes,' I said.

The blow was of such uncontrolled violence that it nearly took my head off. I went backwards to the floor, hitting my head and seeing stars and blackness. I was lifted roughly to my shaky feet and slapped across the face, again and again, and lost consciousness.

When I came to, I found myself bound hand and foot, tied to a chair, and gagged with a dishcloth. There I remained until the baking was done and the kitchen cleaned, hearing Miss Eva murmur over and over again, 'You little thief.' She was beyond all reason.

Suddenly I felt a blow to the back of my head, then another, and another. She was hitting me with a saucepan.

She picked up a knife and I thought it was all up with me. She was going to cut my throat. But it was the string she cut, freeing my arms and legs and all the time jabbering to herself and taking furtive peeps through the door. She opened the door and threw me out into the rain, where I landed in a puddle.

She was standing over me, a broom in her hand, and if I hadn't gotten away she'd have skulled me. I managed to stagger off, dived into the bushes, and crawled into the undergrowth where nobody could find me. Where, oh where, was the White Rabbit and that convenient rabbit-hole?

After a while I decided to get out of the rain and cold and hide in the outside lavatory. I stood there, shaking and shivering, too weak to make another run. Splashy footsteps approached and there were Gwen and the three reptiles, well wrapped up against the weather. I was soundly scolded and made to stand in my knickers and wash myself and my dress. Not until I was perfectly clean was I allowed to change into dry clothing.

At last they left me with Gwen and I told her all that had happened to me. She felt the bumps on my head and could see the bruises on my body and the eye blackening from the slaps about my lace. Shocked by my punishment, she took a risk and made a cup of tea for each of us, but we had to be quick.

We had hardly finished and washed and put away the cups before we heard movements and she slipped quietly away. Secretly I began following her but stopped when I heard voices in one of the rooms forbidden to me. 'Shouldn't we get rid of her?' someone was saying.

Back I went to the kitchen, to sit at the table and pretend to read 'Alice in Wonderland,' my heart in a wonderland of its own at the thought of getting away from this evil place.

After finishing my chores the next day, I went to the kitchen where Gwen was having her breakfast. Every part of me hurt from the beating I had been given. I put my hand on hers to indicate that I had no hard feelings towards her and walked out, aching from head to foot, vowing to starve rather than eat any more of their food.

'The Queen of Hearts, she made some tarts...' and smashed the life out of a defenceless evacuee. Those people prided themselves on being socially superior, educated. They thought themselves gentry. The lower classes they regarded as of unsound mind and in need of their guidance and control. Snobs, they looked down their noses at the people of the village I was helpless in their hands.

Word of my thrashing got back to the billeting officer charged with looking after our welfare, but nothing was done for me. The vicar and his sisters were too prominent in the community.

Chapter 6

Entering the kitchen, I caught them talking to Gwen in their la-di-dah English, the snobby bitches; the moment they saw me, they changed to Welsh so that I should not understand. I turned on my heel and went out for a stroll until Gwen told me that it was safe to return. Little did they know that I was getting a step ahead of them. I already understood quite a lot of Welsh and was secretly learning more fast.

Sunday was their great day. They were on parade and in procession to their place of worship, Christian soldiers onward going. Splash, a bird dropped its load in front of them, but, eyes resolutely front, they neither blinked nor side-stepped but marched on through. But if they had been able to catch that heathen bird shitting on the Lord's day, they would have wrung its neck, that's for sure.

Chapter 7

School holidays were a time of torment for me. Trapped in the rigorous religious routine of a church household, Gwen and I had to attend morning prayers in the dining room, where we sat around the standing vicar as he pontificated on whatever happened to come into his holy mind. On and on it went, punctuated by his sisters' trance-like moanings of 'Yes' and 'Yeeas.' These sessions might begin as early as 8:30 a.m. and go on for two long, crazy hours or more. They ought to have invited the whole village to their Old Time Cranks' Show.

I adopted what looked like the posture of someone at prayer, my fingers splayed over my eyes. I squinted through the gaps to spy on the devotional fools, made pretend binoculars to zoom in on their conscientiously devout faces, and studied the vicar's fishlike mouth as it opened and closed and silently to mimic his outpourings.

Nobody was permitted to leave the room, no matter how urgent her need for the toilet. I was often desperate; my bladder swelled like a balloon ready to burst, and it was a race, when at last the session came to its end, to get relief before wetting myself. What would Alice have done, I wondered, as I baptised the pedestal with outpourings of pee.

My Sunday morning breakfast was bacon and dried eggs. There were plenty of fresh eggs in the cupboard, but they were reserved for family. At no time while I was their guest did I enjoy the luxury of a fresh boiled egg. Here was my week's menu:

> Monday: One plate porridge, bread, butter and a cup of tea
> Tuesday: Bacon, fried bread (soggy), bread and butter, tea
> Wednesday: Bread and butter, one teaspoonful jam, tea
> Thursday—Sunday: Mean variations on the above.

I cannot remember having cheese at any time (they said it gave you indigestion). The family had substantial meals, and what they comprised I was never allowed to discover. I know that I couldn't digest the prayers that invariably followed.

In the wider world beyond our isolated village the war increased its ferocity: servicemen killed, homes bombed, Coventry levelled. Meanwhile, the vicar and his sisters made my life hell and worshipped the god they were supposed to believe had loved us so much that he died for us. I was forced the read the Bible until I was sick to death of it, and I would have made a bonfire of the damned thing if I could. Alice was my salvation and Lewis Carroll's books my holy writ. Over and over again I read her whimsical adventures and worshipped the colourful characters she met. In my own little imaginary world, I was Alice.

One dry morning the three sisters went on safari to collect moss, from which it was said iodine would be extracted for the forces. I walked behind, carrying the cardboard box. On and on we walked, miles and miles, it seemed to me, and I noticed that these women always took care never to tread on each other's shadows. Were they sacred? Holy ghosts?

The vicar seldom left the house. He moved about it in silence, broken only by the mice in his shoes, a creeping Jesus if ever there was one. We hardly knew he was there unless we heard the taps running. Like

Pontius Pilate, he was a great hand washer: We would hear him at it at intervals throughout the day.

Cleanliness is next to godliness, they say, but it's a poor substitute for that quality! 'Take no notice of him, *cariad*,' Gwen used to say.

At school one day, loud shouting broke out at the front of the classroom. The teacher had smacked a girl and a furious boy was yelling, 'Leave my sister be, you bitch.' Things got out of hand very quickly. He attacked Miss Jones, biting and kicking until she had to take refuge in another room. A vicious row followed when the parents came to take their children home; Miss Jones wisely stayed well out of sight until they had gone.

On another occasion, one beautiful day a gang of us evacuees were happily walking down a hilly lane when we heard the most terrifying screams from behind a farm shed. The horror of them froze our blood, and our lovely day was torn apart. Terrified, we covered our ears, but the screams echoed through and there was no place to hide.

We ran for help, our legs like jelly, to a neighbouring cottage, but when we knocked on the door the man who appeared just said, 'It's only an old pig having his throat cut.' This, then, was the reality of idyllic country life, this barbarous act of cruel men. Did people scream when their throats were cut, I wondered I prayed to God I'd never hear those awful sounds again, nor feel the sense of guilt that accompanied them.

I had another nasty experience at a farm where they had a sty full of lovely piglets. I was so taken with them that I asked the farmer's wife if I could go in and see them.

'Why yes,' she said, 'do go and have a look if you want to.' The floor of the sty was deep in straw in which the attractive babies romped around their hulking mother. But from the straw, to my horror, a rat's face peeped out. Searching for something to frighten it away, I noticed, in the straw near the wall, what I took to be a stick. But when I picked it up there was a loud snap and a terrible pain in my left hand.

I had picked up the trap set to catch the rats, and blood was pouring from my fingers. I screamed and made a huge effort not to faint, believing that if I were to do so the rats would eat me alive. Lifting the trap I carried it into the house, where the farmer's wife released my hand and washed and dressed my wounds. I was extremely lucky not to have had my fingers taken off.

There was no mercy for me back at the vicarage. 'Stupid little worm! See what happens when you disobey us.' One might have thought the doctor would be called, or that they might have taken me along for a check-up. Nothing of the kind! Miss Elen roughly pulled the temporary bandages off and the tears burned my eyes from her rough treatment. 'Keep your hand still, do you hear!' she shouted into my ear. Don't every go near that piggery again. Pigs eat worms like you.'

It felt as if she was tearing my fingers off. What she really did was to pour raw disinfectant over the wound and re-bandage it tightly. The pain of this torture, which I'm sure she enjoyed, made me jump and writhe. As soon as I could get away I ran to a roadside tap and put my bandaged hand under the strong flow of cold water to dilute the burning disinfectant. Then I re-bandaged myself and the relief was great.

I knew Mum was doing war-work somewhere, in a munitions factory, perhaps, but because of the bombing she had to move more than once and I never heard from her. Fortunately I had her old letters to read and re-read and feel that I was still her beloved daughter.

My friends and I loved to roam the countryside, and on one woodland walk we came on what appeared to be a summer snowfall. A single track of footprints led across the white carpet, and we wondered whether Father Christmas had come out of hibernation early this year. But the 'snowfall' was a layer of petals from the avenue of blackthorn trees that we were walking through. With delight we kicked the petals into the air and threw handfuls at each other, just as if it really had been snow. It was an enormous delight to our girlish nature.

The arctic track led us into a farmyard with a large barn. There was a farm worker there, rather shy and very surprised to see us. He was not too surprised to tease, though, and told us that among the lofty beams of the barn lived rats which mated with the bats up there. The bats, he told us, were very bad-tempered and if disturbed they would fly around hitting people. We were looking up in awe to see these pugnacious creatures when he made us jump by shouting. 'Here's one coming to bite you all. Run!'

In our panic we slipped in the cow muck and got into a dreadfully stinking mess before we picked ourselves up and ran back the way we had come. We were so ignorant about the countryside and its ways. The dangerous bird in the rafters was really a harmless owl.

We stopped at a stream to wash our nice dresses, shoes and socks. Then we walked on in burning sunshine in just our knickers, vests and shoes, waving our dresses and socks in the warm air to dry them. By the time we reached the village they were quite dry. We had made ourselves respectable again and nobody ever knew about our learning experience.

Each Thursday a social evening was put on for us. Nobody was allowed in unless he or she was wearing black shoes. On one particular Thursday, I turned up in brown shoes and was told to go back and change them. I did not want to return to the vicarage unnecessarily, so I sneaked out the back, took off the brown shoes, and reappeared in my black socks. Nobody noticed at first.

A feature of the evening was a competition with a prize of threepence for the winner. I entered and won. But then my black socks were noticed and I was disqualified. Everyone had a good laugh at my cheek, which made me feel uncomfortable. In compensation I was awarded a farthing and the title of Joker of the Evening.

In the very middle of the village great clumps of brambles grew in a boggy area. In the soggiest parts were to be found delicious giant juicy blackberries, which we ate by the handful. One day, we were working our way carefully towards some even juicier berries when from behind some low bushes arose a witch-like woman in a voluminous blue frock and white apron. Bedraggled hair hung down to her shoulders and she screamed, 'I'll catch you! I'll catch you!' and stretched out long arms and hands with claws for fingers.

Panic-stricken at the sight and sound of this wild-eyed creature of the bogs, we struggled knee-deep through the mire to solid ground and escaped over the hedge, hearts leaping like yo-yos. We never did get as many blackberries as we would have liked, but we never dared again enter the domain of the Blackberry Witch.

On Tuesday evenings I was given 'Woman's Weekly' to read, but it was often snatched out of my hands before I had finished the latest episode of the Adventures of Roley and Rosemary. One day it was noticed that I was reading other parts of the magazine and, out of sheer spite, these pages were cut out, leaving me just the serial. I looked on Roley and Rosemary as my pals, and was very glad to be able to read something about them once a week.

One day all hell broke loose at the vicarage. Tensions shook the place to its very foundations when an agitated woman who would not take no for an answer managed to force her way in. It was no business of mine, but of course I longed to know who she was and what she had come for, this fierce cat among the vicarage pigeons. There were sounds of furniture being thrown about, raised voices, inflamed passions. Was it a family row? The disturbance went on and on, with high voices crying out and unholy screams that threatened to bring the roof down on all our heads.

This went on for three whole days, but all was kept out of my sight. Gwen made herself scarce, neglected the housework, and as soon as she saw me coming home from school she took me out with her and stayed out with me until it was time for me to go to bed. Then I had a taste of supper and was packed off.

At last, on the Saturday morning, the front door slammed and I caught a glimpse of an elegantly dressed lady walking down the path. This was the mysterious cause of all the mayhem. From her behaviour she must surely, I thought, be a close relation of the three bitches, and I had a feeling that she would be back again one day to give them another taste of their own medicine. How I longed to meet her!

So distressed in body and spirit were the sisters, and so much mess was there to clean up, that only the vicar went to divine worship that Sunday. A cloud of gloom hung over the house, and it was days before discipline was restored and another ghastly Sunday was upon us. Three times that day I was made to go to church, under strict supervision, marched between

Miss Beti and Miss Elen, silent and upright as besoms. Daft Miss Eva stayed behind to prepare meals.

I wanted to dance a protest all over the road in my tight, squeaking shoes, but I was kept in line by the scruff of my neck and with stem reproof. When we met local people, they would greet us in Welsh, but the sisters would reply in English to demonstrate their superiority. They always walked close to the walls of the houses for fear someone might tread on their sacred shadows.

In our pew I was trapped between the two of them and supposed to keep rigidly silent and still all service long. Any infringement was punished by a kick on the ankle. I passed the boring minutes by making imaginary changes in the appearance of members of the congregation, a different hat for this one, a different dress for that, an alternative hairstyle or no hair at all. I imagined Miss Beti and Miss Elen to have grown cows' horns and to be mooing the hymns. Nobody seemed to realise the torment a child undergoes when forced to endure the monotony of adult worship.

Chapter 8

I suffered another blow when Gwen, the buffer between me and my three enemies, left to join up. My world was falling apart. I could only dread a future without her support. I was sure that seeing my maltreatment was what had driven her away.

A strange letter arrived from Mum. It did not seem to be in her handwriting and it explained nothing. Had she been injured? Why was it so short, hardly worth writing at all? And if someone was impersonating Mum, how did they know my address?

Being separated from my beloved mother was the darkest time of my life, a period during which, I believe, I was hardly sane. My mind dwelt frequently on the things of home. Was she taking care of my Shirley Temple dress, socks, and shoes that I loved so much? They were very special to me because she had

had to get them made privately at considerable expense. Would they be there waiting for me when I returned home?

What about Rosie, my dead sister's doll, whom I had named after her when she became mine? I had left her behind, and her companions, the golliwog with the bright, smiling face and the smaller doll dressed in black. Were they still sitting where I had left them, on the chair in my bedroom, waiting for me to come home and comfort them?

With aching heart I wrote, again and again, to Mum and got no real replies. One or two evasive letters came, but in somebody else's writing. I was trapped in a quagmire of doubt and conflicting thoughts. 'Dear Mum, where are you? What are you doing? Have you forgotten me? Please answer me.'

How I wished that Gwen could have taken me along with her to the WRENS. Isolation was destroying me, that and my meagre diet. My food, such as it was, was left for me on the kitchen table by a person or persons unknown. If I wanted a second cup of tea, the palaver involved in getting it was too much—knock gently on the door of the living room, return to my chair, wait. . . and wait. . . and wait. And eventually be called in to place my cup on their table, eyes submissively lowered, then take the filled cup back to the kitchen, never once raising my eyes to theirs.

What a thrill they got from tormenting me! Finally it became too much for me to ask any favours and I was off to bed at half-past seven sharp. I used to sit on the bed, eyes closed but afraid to go to sleep, because if I did the change of position would wake me up.

Once I awoke to find myself in the kitchen—I had been sleepwalking. My heart raced: how often had I done this without remembering? I crept on tiptoe back up the stairs in a state of nervous desperation.

One day a tide of excitement raced through the children of the village. A rare ration of sweets had come into the shops. I ran breathless all the way to the vicarage to get my coupons and money. The weird sisters turned their backs on my excitement, and by the time one ghoul had got the coupons and another the money, the sweets were sold out and I wept in disappointment.

All was not lost, though, because it was thought that a shop near the beach had sweets. There was a race to get there before they too were sold out, and again I came last and all were gone.

In my desperation I surprised myself by saying, to the old lady who kept the shop, '*Os gwelwch yn dda a oes melysion gyda chi?*' ('Please, have you got any sweets?')

On hearing this, she called me into her back room, made me sit down, gave me sweets from her reserve supply, and explained, 'I want to reward you for speaking to me in Welsh. And I want you to do so every time you come here. I shall keep some sweets for you, only for you, you understand, and not a word to the other children.'

Then this dear old lady brought down from a shelf a large cardboard box and from it took out the biggest bar of milk chocolate I had ever seen. 'This is for you,' she said. 'And not a word to anyone else. Promise me, now.' My life being what it then was, such kindness completely overwhelmed me. Tears ran down my face. If I stayed longer I'd flood the shop with my weeping. *'Diolch yn fawr'* ('Thank you very much'), I managed to say, and ran off to the beach to be alone.

I kept my bar of chocolate hidden under my armpit inside my dress and ran as fast as I knew how to find the most sheltered corner of the beach. There I sat down to enjoy the feast of a lifetime. A stray dog wandered along and sat beside me, looking up expectantly with brown eyes. I gave him a share, and surely no happier couple had ever graced this beach. I ate slowly, savouring every morsel, and I believe the dog did the same. There was still a lot left when I walked back to the village, followed by the dog, to whom I surreptitiously gave a few more pieces of chocolate.

A more serious sensation occurred when scarlet fever broke out and spread like wildfire. There were no isolation hospitals in this rural area to contain it, and I caught it. According to my wardens, I wasn't ill enough—again—for the doctor to be called in, but I was certainly ill. Each night I suffered bouts of fever and felt, in my delirium, that I was wrestling with unseen forces. The welcome light of morning would reveal bedclothes in tangled confusion and damp with the sweats of the night. I must have had a very strong constitution, for I recovered eventually without treatment of any kind.

One day I was about to have my tea in the kitchen when it occurred to me that it was customary to say grace before meals. So 'Thank the Lord,' I said, 'for what I've had, a little more would make me glad!' I ought to have known better than to have supposed I could do anything in private in that house, for the door burst open and there, listening, were the three ghouls. 'You little twitter,' they said. 'That's no grace, it's a blasphemous disgrace. Shame on you!'

'You've no right to listen in on me,' I replied at once. 'Haven't you anything better to do with your time?'

'Ungrateful little bitch,' came the reply. 'If we had our way we'd....' I broke in, 'You know you'd never get another evacuee. People know all about your evil ways. That's why Gwen left.'

I expected a hiding, but although they huffed and puffed, they thought better of it and left, slamming the door behind them. But I was getting deeper and deeper into their bad books. And there was more, much more to come.

Every Sunday, of course, we all had to go to Sunday school. Our teacher there was a stern, unpleasant, bullying woman. One day she hit me across the face in front of the whole class. Humiliated, but very angry, without hesitation I hit her back and then, to everyone's amazement, we were fighting on the floor, her big black bloomers on public display. The rest of the class laughed and cheered until we were pulled apart.

A shocked silence followed because everybody knew that for a child to come to blows with the best Sunday school teacher the church had ever had was a sacrilege, a profanity. Stories soon spread through the village about this wild evacuee who had hurled the teacher over the pews and jumped on her.

The three sisters were outraged and called me before their inquisition. Loud verbal explosions boomed about my ears. They had never heard of, could not have imagined, such behaviour in THEIR church.

'You are a devil-girl,' they said. 'Fighting in our God's House. We are all of us degraded by the way you behave.'

'I didn't realise,' said I, 'that the church was YOUR house. Everyone else says that it's God's.'

'Aren't you ashamed of yourself? And to answer back like that. You are ruining the Reverend James's reputation, making us the talk of the village.'

'You deserve to burn in hell,' said Miss Beti.

'To me,' said Miss Eva, elegantly, 'you are nothing other than the hole under the donkey's tail. We no longer want you in our house.'

When they ran out of breath at last, I said. 'I am not going to let ANYONE slap me around and get away with it. She had no right to hit me across the face. Nor have any of you.'

There were butterflies a-plenty in my stomach when I appeared in public again, but both children and adults congratulated me on standing up for myself. Even members of the church congregation were divided. A lot of people came out of curiosity to see this wild foreign kitten who had caused such agitation and rumpus. People would pat me on the back or head and say, 'Good girl!' To many I was the heroine of the day.

Next Sunday the church was fuller than usual. People had come to see me, and the sisters were very much embarrassed. In the chapels there was talk of David and Goliath and a good deal of pleasure at this scandal afflicting the Church in Wales.

A few weeks later, after some church meeting which we had to attend, we children were standing around outside when someone mentioned that if you walked anti-clockwise seven times round the church and stopped by the door, the devil himself would appear. Always ready for a dare, a group of us decided to try it. Round and round we walked, and the seventh time, just as we reached the door, who should emerge but the Reverend James in his long black clothes. We hastily made ourselves scarce and never repeated the experiment in case we got Satan himself next time.

At last my constitution was starting to give way under the pressure of my miserable life and especially from my lack of proper sleep. In school I was quite unable to concentrate on the lessons, and almost every day I was punished by being made to stand out in front of the class. I was so wobbly on my feet that it was hard to prevent myself from falling over.

On one occasion, as I sat in my desk, my head became so heavy with drowsiness that it fell uncontrollably forward with a loud thump on the desk lid. I passed out and they gave me a drink of water and escorted me quietly to the cloakroom, where I was allowed to sit in peace by myself. When they came back to see how I was, I was fast asleep on the floor.

The teachers became more worried about me. Thinking that there must be something seriously wrong, they called in the doctor. Discussions began behind the scenes about my welfare. Nearly a million and a half children had been evacuated, and more than half of them had been returned to their homes; why hadn't I?

Sunday again, and time for the collection. Up and down went the sidesman until he came to a well-dressed woman sitting alone. To the astonishment of the entire congregation she gathered up the coins in the plate, carefully counted them, then dropped the majority into her handbag. Then she placed a one pound note on the plate and waved it on. We children could hardly stop ourselves laughing aloud.

Afterwards, running along the lane at play, we came on two men digging a hole. 'What's that hole for?' we asked.

'We're going to bury Mr Big, if you want to know,' one of them said, winking at the other.

'Who's Mr Big, then?'

'Go and ask the vicar. He'll be along any time now.'

'But we're asking you.'

'We-e-l-l, if your sharp noses are that long, I'll tell you. It's an elephant.'

We stared at them, wondering how so large a beast could be fitted into such a small hole, then off we ran. Ask a silly question....

We walked on between the tree-lined hedgerows where branches made an arch over the lane. What was that splashing noise? It wasn't raining, and there was no stream here. Then we saw some local boys among the trees, backs turned to the road. 'Pissy pigs!' we chanted, 'Pissy pigs,' and ran away as fast as we could or we'd have had a thumping.

As we passed some roadside cottages we heard a group of gossiping women refer to us as 'plant y sais' and, more affectionately, 'plant bach y sais' ('children of the English' or 'the little English children'). How much better than the usual 'evacuees.' The boys were after us, though. We could hear the sound of their heavy boots on the road. They were gaining. How were we to escape? Luckily we saw an open front door and were able to step quietly into the passage out of sight and then run back the way we had come once our pursuers were out of sight.

As we again passed the men digging the hole, they shouted, 'Send the vicar along. We're ready to bury the elephant.'

'Bury it yourselves,' we shouted back.

There were fewer and fewer natural, happy moments like this for me, though. My mental state was getting worse. The next Sunday, as the congregation came out of church and stood about to gossip, I heard Mum's voice. It was an awful moment. I froze in my tracks and my heart seemed to stop beating. I would have known Mum's voice anywhere. Where was she?

In a panic, I circled around, desperately looking for her. Had she come, at last, to take me home? But fate and my disturbed state had played a cruel trick on me. The voice belonged to a stranger. I had only imagined that it was Mum's.

In class the following day I became unconscious, and nothing the teachers were able to do would wake me up. I was put in the cloakroom, laid across some forms and the doctor was sent for again. He managed to wake me up, and he gave me a check-up. He could find nothing physically wrong.

'I think what she needs is untroubled rest,' he said. 'Let her sleep as long as she wants to and I'll come back and see her again tomorrow.' In the fleeting seconds before I lost consciousness again, I heard the worried teachers talking about the billeting officer.

I slept all day. Evacuee girls took turns watching over me. About a week later, as I was sitting again in class, dreaming of what I would do in the summer holidays which were about to begin, I was asked to return to the vicarage. Slowly I got my school things together, wondering what I had done wrong this time. Things were not as they should be; surely they were going to accuse me of something terrible.

When we got there, I saw a car parked outside and. standing beside it, the billeting officer. I was not allowed to enter the vicarage or speak to anyone. Things were happening so fast that I could not understand. Surely he had not come to take me away? I looked into the car and saw all my belongings were there. 'What's happening,' I asked. 'Where are you taking me?'

'Please get into the car now,' he said. 'I'll explain later.'

There were no farewells, thank God, and nobody came out to see me go. Stunned and disoriented, as we drove away I could not even feel happy to have escaped. He told me that, for medical reasons, a change of billets was essential. The truth began to dawn on me. I was free at last.

Goodbye, creepy vicarage! Goodbye, ghouls! Goodbye and good riddance!

Chapter 9

To my surprise, we didn't go beyond the village, only to the billeting hostel in a side-street at the far end of a long, long road. I carried in my belongings and met the nurse-in-charge, who had been forewarned of my arrival and the reasons for it. There were eight evacuees there of my age or older, and eight younger children, sixteen of us in all. None of them would be allowed to take my place at the vicarage.

Although still in a state of shock at the suddenness of my move, I was delighted to have constant company of children my own age after the cold loneliness I had suffered so long. It was unreal. I had to pinch myself to believe what was happening to me.

The food was so good. Plenty of rich-tasting cawl (soup-stew), such a change from mean solitary meals in the vicarage kitchen. Here I was surrounded with smiling faces and happy chatter. Tired out but overjoyed, I relished every moment.

The happy-faced cook always had a cheerful and humorous word for me and did everything possible to make all of us feel at home. What freedom, what a relief from the constant tensions of the vicarage—it was like a resurrection.

There was one fly in the ointment, though. The hostel was only a temporary refuge until another billet became available.

I never wanted to go to church again, but attendance was compulsory. I never had to encounter the ghoulish sisters, though, because we were taken in turn to each of the chapels in the neighbourhood.

Three weeks passed like a summer holiday and we were told that some of us would be leaving for billets in local homes. I could not face another strange house; this hostel and its happy company suited me down to the ground.

Moreover, I was very worried about the night-horrors that continued to haunt me. At first my screams had frightened my fellow evacuees, but they had gotten used to them.

Every night I tried my hardest not to drop off to sleep, walking about the room, looking out of the window, anything to avoid the nightmares. One night I saw, emerging from the derelict house opposite, a dark lady dressed in a voluminous skirt and with a cape over her shoulders. She walked carefully and slowly a little way down the road, stopped, looked around and crossed two doors down from the hostel. At this point, where once a house had stood, she disappeared. I was not frightened, though. She would have been very welcome at my bedside after the three ghouls, but I never trusted myself to look out of the window again at night.

I had thought that here, in company, I should be able to sleep easy, but no sooner did I fall asleep than I would find myself in convulsions, my legs kicking off all the bedclothes. How would this kind of behaviour go down in my new family?

It was a pleasure, though, to walk about the village. No more evacuee school. I even dared to speak Welsh of a sort to people I met in the street, and they were very patient with me. There were adventures, too — evacuees walked in where angels feared to tread.

Playing in high spirits on the coastal path one day, careless of my surroundings, I suddenly found myself on the edge of a cliff. Seagulls soared above and below the echoing sea lashed sharp rocks. My head reeled, and I stumbled and fell. Only by clutching desperately at a thick tuft of grass did I save myself from going over. Slowly I edged back from the brink, shaking from head to foot. I then lay there, out of breath, gazing up into the beautiful blue sky. I was safe, but below the remains of sheep hung rotting on the jagged rocks.

One day I was called in to a tiny office and told that I was just the right person to be companion to a baby girl with very busy parents. I pleaded with the billeting officer to let me stay at the hostel. 'I never want to leave here,' I said, 'except to go home to Mum. I'm frightened to go elsewhere. Please let me stay.'

'I'm afraid it's impossible, my dear child,' he said, kindly. This hostel is for temporary accommodation only. Nobody is permanent here, and when we've found places for all of you, it will close.' His voice was full of concern.

There was nothing for it but to do as I was told. I was the only suitable candidate and plans had already been made. A few days later, I said my goodbyes to those few of my companions who remained. There would be no more happy meals or walks, and I should sorely miss all the friends that I had made.

My nerves knotted tight as the car drew up outside the hostel. Confused and unhappy, I couldn't speak.

'You'll be all right,' said the billeting officer, cheerfully, 'just you wait and see. Everything is going to turn out for the best.'

We drove for what seemed miles along twisting roads that ran through beautiful countryside. The car seemed to hit every pothole in the road, but I was even jumpier than it was.

At long last we stopped outside a tiny public house at a crossroads. It looked claustrophobic to me, closed in by high hedgerows among a network of creepy by-roads. An elderly woman came out to meet us, accompanied by a younger woman, her married daughter.

We were taken down to the dark back-kitchen, where the warm atmosphere was very welcoming. Here we sat down and the billeting officer chatted with the women. After a brief conversation he got up, patted me on the head and said, 'You will be well looked after here, and I shall not fail to call in from time to time and see how you're settling in. Goodbye for now.'

He was gone, and immediately a nice warm meal was put before me. But I was too scared to eat or talk: my knees were knocking. But the women were very patient with me, and gradually the barriers fell away.

'The billeting officer has told us a little about you,' they said, 'and we are very pleased to welcome you among us. All we ask of you is to give us a try and to make yourself right at home here. He tells us that you can speak a little Welsh, which is a good thing because most of our customers are Welsh-speakers.'

'My name is Beryl...'

'Yes, we know,' said the younger woman, gently. 'And this is my mother, Mrs Davies, but we call her Mari fach. And my name is Bessi, and my baby — you'll meet her later, she's sleeping in her pram at the moment — is Rosemary.'

They took me on a conducted tour. At the back of the pub was a garden and orchard, and at the bottom of this the ty bach, or dry toilet. They showed me my bedroom, which overlooked the crossroads, then left me to myself.

When evening came there was a riot of noisy conversations in the bar and, later, the sound of glasses smashing on the floor. It was a very eventful evening for me, and it was a long time before I could get to sleep in the new atmosphere.

Next morning I met Rosemary for the first time. She was a lovely baby, wide awake and giggling. I loved her at once, and she was my companion all day long. Mari fach and Bessi were too busy at their work to disturb us. In the evening, to my alarm, Bessi took me into the crowded bar. *'Dyma Beryl,'* she said, *'yr ifacwi sy wedi dod i aros gyda ni. Rhoiwch croeso mawr iddi, a dim siarad saesneg, ond cymraeg.'* ('This is Beryl, the evacuee who has come to stay with us. Give her a warm welcome and speak no English to her, only Welsh.' Then she added that the drink was on the house.

I shied away, embarrassed by all the strange faces looking at me, feeling like a freak in a side-show. Afterwards I felt as exhausted as a run-down battery.

When night fell out here in the remote countryside it was darker than Hades, total blackout. Mari fach took me by the arm and led me into the back-kitchen for a homely chat by the fire. A bold-faced old grandfather clock, smoke-stained, ticked away the silence. Soon the regular customers began to drift in and we had to move up the bench to make room for them. It was time for me to go to bed as the inn filled up.

Army convoys shook my windows as I prepared for bed. Mari fach went to her own room at the back of the house, while Bessi served the rowdy customers downstairs. It was hard work for her; she had to be everywhere at the same time.

Below my bedroom was the entrance to the pub, giving onto a passage that went most of the way through the building. At the far end, on the left, was a serving hatch giving access to the crowded bar. Men's noisy voices were separated from my bedroom by no more than the thickness of a plank. It was very hard to get to sleep over the bedlam of what sounded to me like a riot breaking out below.

These kind people gave me plenty of time to settle in and find my own place. After a week or so, I was accepted as one of the family and felt thoroughly at home. It was time to think about my education again. I would attend the village school about half a mile away. How would the children take to me, I wondered.

Life at the pub was blessed freedom to me. No questions were asked, no restrictions placed on me. I went where I pleased, ate as I pleased and was allowed, within reason, to stay up as long as I pleased. Blessed freedom and never a dull moment. No solitary confinements, no endless eerie silence, and no formality. Everyone here was known by a nickname, and the people of the house were too preoccupied with earning a living to be self-absorbed. Best of all, there was no religion to torment me.

The pub was strategically placed at its crossroads. There was a stop outside for the ancient buses that rolled and swayed the roads like the stagecoaches of a Welsh Fargo. These bus routes were the lifelines of the west: they linked the villages with the towns, the hillside communities with those of the valleys.

The pub had a fine reputation for its hospitality and the quality of its beer. Passengers and goods of all sorts were dropped off or picked up here: letters, parcels, live and dead poultry, children, medicines and shopping. The only thing missing were six-shooters, shotguns, and outlaws.

Alice would certainly have approved of my new world. I thought it better than her world: its characters might sometimes be grotesque, but they were real. The kings of the roads were the drivers and conductors of the buses. The local people had known each other from birth, and their relationships were affectionate. Mari fach was something between a goddess and a mother to me. Bustling about in her brilliant starched apron, always with an infectious smile, she made her many tasks seem like fun and was always ready with good advice about any problem I might have.

The sun shone every day for Mari. Her body might be getting old, but her spirit was youthful as a child's. It was she who did all the cooking: delicious cakes, pies and tarts. The most appetising smells in the world drifted constantly from her kitchen, fragrances to draw angels out of heaven.

I felt myself on the threshold of another and broader life-, anticipating so many new interesting and delightful experiences that a passion of radiant well-being possessed me. I was trusted to take baby Rosemary out for walks in her pram, and I loved her baby laughter and being alone with her in the beautiful countryside.

Then came the day when I got back from our morning walk and, after Mari fach had taken the baby off to be fed, Bessi asked me to sit by her. She took my hand gently in hers. As our eyes met in a moment of silence, I thought I was going to faint. My happiness was coming to an end: she was going to tell me bad news. Was I going to be sent back to the hostel? The ticking of the grandfather clock seemed unnaturally loud. It was ticking my doom, I was sure of it.

Bessi saw the fear in my eyes and broke the spell. 'We're very glad to have found you; you're the right girl for us and we hope you'll want to stay here. The bad things that happened to you in the past will never happen here.'

Overwhelmed at being spoken to with such open kindness, I could not believe my luck. I stared at her, tongue-tied, wondering what the billeting officer had told her. She kissed me on the forehead and said, 'Beryl fach, have no fear of us. Just be one of the family and make yourself at home.' Then she hurried away: there was no time here for idle chatter because there was always work to do.

In spite of the kindness of Bessi and her mother, I continued to be plagued by deep anxieties and tensions. The night-horrors were still with me, and I was afraid that my kind friends would find them too much to put up with and send me away. But nothing was said in the mornings, when all the doors stood open and fresh air blew away the stink of beer and tobacco. Mari fach and Bessi mopped and swept and dusted until everything was clean and gleaming, especially the smooth and polished bar.

Saturday was not their favourite day because it was on Saturday mornings that their most disgusting customer used to make his regular visit. He was addicted to chewing tobacco, and between gulps of beer he would cough up clots of phlegm and abundant tobacco juice and spit this onto the newly cleaned floor. He would sit there for hours, sipping his pints of beer, spitting, and loudly farting. When he left, the floor would be in such a mess that no other customer would enter the bar until it had been cleaned up again. They called him the Beast from the Beyond.

Mornings were the best times because they were so peaceful after the noise of the evenings. In spite of the noise, this was a strict house. Bessi was intolerant of drunken fools and no horseplay or fighting was tolerated. The men were given plenty of leeway, but if they ever went too far they got their marching orders at once.

Whenever customers were heard speaking to me in English, Bessi would remind them to speak only in Welsh. Soon my command of Welsh had improved so much that I was speaking to them like a local and able to understand the stories of all the wonderful things that were happening around the countryside. All the choicest gossip, all the juiciest rumours circulated in our bar, and there was plenty of talk about current affairs and wise comment on the progress of the war.

When my night-horrors continued to cause me to wake with terrified screams, it was Mari fach who came to hold and comfort me. Far from wishing to get rid of me as a nuisance, she was endlessly patient and sat with me many a night, giving me comfort and reassurance.

Bessi took her turn also, and would sit by me, embracing me and smoothing my hair. I cannot find the words to express my love and gratitude to these kind, humane friends who made me feel one of their family and comforted me in my loneliness and pain.

Not even Alice could have imagined the wonderland I now found myself enjoying, once I had got into the swing of the rowdy world of the pub. There were so many fascinating real characters to enjoy, and it became a pleasure to listen to the men singing such songs as 'There's a devil in the beer-barrel so they say....' I was becoming Welsh in thought, word, and deed.

In the kitchen corner, near the fire, was a small space into which I could fit snugly and out of everyone's way. This became for me a kind of listening post from which, unnoticed, I heard strange confessions, bizarre experiences, the overflowing of hearts and minds beset with love and marriage problems.

I acquired discretion: to hear confidential matters and not repeat them, to see sights and never tell anyone about them, to learn the lesson of the Three Wise Monkeys. The warm, homely back-kitchen served as an unofficial social centre where discreet people met, not necessarily for a drink but to talk business or seek advice on social or family problems. I heard a great deal and passed nothing on.

If the weather was fine on a Sunday, I would take Rosemary for walks. One day I took her to the local church, a few hundred yards up the road. She loved the singing, but carried on babbling after the hymn had finished. I could not help giggling at her antics, but the vicar's face was red with embarrassment and I was told off for bringing a young child into the church and disturbing the congregation at their devotions. After this we took our walks on the lonely by-ways.

It was a help to Bessi and Mari fach to have us out of the way while they did the cleaning, and there was no need to hurry back. On a Sunday we could have our meals whenever we liked.

What I enjoyed most of all, now that I could understand Welsh, was to listen to the Fireside Philosophers. These old men would gather in the back-kitchen, where they showed great skill in debating important matters and telling stories. They were all the more impressive because they never raised their voices as they mulled over the deaths and births in the district, the omens and eerie aspects of life.

They told stories too, the ancient myths and legends of their country, bringing their imagery to life with expressive gestures and outstretched fingers that pointed like magic wands. These old men, and their fund of traditional knowledge and wisdom were dying out even then, and now are no more. It was a great privilege for me to have known them and been given entry to their world of common sense, romance, and magic.

Chapter 10

I couldn't remember seeing many military uniforms in my previous village, but this one, especially in the evenings, was full of them; American soldiers, R.A.F., army, navy, land girls, nurses. Civilians came in also, from the humble labourer to top scientists from the nearby experimental establishments.

A local wit remarked in the bar that the only ones who did not come in search of pleasure were the dead, and that not for want of trying—he had seen the goings-on in the graveyard, the courting couples rising from the tombstones after their love-making.

'There's a lot of shaky women round here,' a friend replied. I had no idea what he meant by 'shaky' but I had seen servicemen giving the wink to English land girls and then going off into the darkness 'for a walk.' It was pitch-black: What on earth was there for them to see?

The accents of many nations echoed in our bar, but laughter sounded the same in any language. Sometimes we had drunken gypsies in, always aggressive, shouting and ready for a fight. Ben, the blacksmith, came too, a jovial man, larger than life unless his sullen wife accompanied him, when he was sadly shrunk. She nagged and abused him mercilessly. After she was gone he would say, 'The old sow's on at me again!' Ben was responsible for repairs of all kinds to carts and wagons and of course for shoeing horses and ponies. As he worked, he would talk to his customers about his experiences, always careful to avoid giving offence.

The gypsies were a rowdy lot even sober, and when they brought their ponies in to be shod, you could hear them a mile away, bragging about their physical strength and laughing at their own jokes. When the work was over, Ben was more or less obliged to accompany them to their camping-ground for a meal and a few drinks. He enjoyed escaping from his wife, however, and raising hell for an hour or two after a hard day of hot, physical work. When she came looking for him next morning, he would excuse himself by saying that he had had to work late and had slept in the smithy.

Ben's wife was a small woman, but he was very much in awe of her. Knowing this, the gypsy women asked whether he would like them to put a curse on her.

'No, no,' he said. Then, 'Well, maybe . . . just a little one. Can you do that?'

It seemed as if they had, for she became meek as a lamb and nice as pie. Somebody had tipped her off that the gypsies were ready to put a nasty curse on her unless she changed her ways. She was terrified of these witch-like women when they came calling, but they were really no different from the women of the village. It was just the act they put on.

Ben took full advantage of the new regime. With a few pints inside him he was the life and soul of the party, a fine speaker, a good singer, and an excellent raconteur who loved to have happy people around him. But when the gypsies moved on, their effect soon wore off, and his wife was back to watching his every move so that he had to sneak into the bar for the occasional secret pint again.

When the doctor was out on his rounds, patients from surrounding farms would gather in the back room to be examined. The doctor himself got free drinks, his favourite tipple being gin and hot water.

After his 'surgery' was over he would sit by the kitchen fire, chatting with friends.

One day he was speaking to Mari fach about the problems with her bladder when the conversation got round to the terrible nightmares that the evacuee girl was having. There was, in his experience, nothing much anybody could do, he said, certainly nothing he could prescribe except patient loving care and frequent reassurance. He had been a medical officer in World War I and knew all about shell-shock and other similar traumas.

'The child has had some terrifying experiences,' he said. 'Taken away from her loving home and family, set among strangers alone. A lot depends on you, now. She needs plenty of love and plenty of activity. Luckily there's always plenty going on here to take her mind off her wounds. She will never forget them, and I doubt if she will ever fully recover, but with love and support she will learn to cope.'

Although there was a small school not far from the pub, for some reason I was sent to a larger one farther away in another village. This was before free school meals were introduced, so I took sandwiches and a bottle of pop. Later, hot, appetizing meals were provided in return for a small fee and served in the infants' classroom.

All of the children were local except for three evacuees. Every child there spoke Welsh, but they were taught in English, a crazy system that would not be changed for a long time yet.

I could easily get to school by bus, for one passed between the door of the pub and the school gates, but unless it was raining heavily I preferred to walk. There was so much to see in the country: foxes and badgers in the undergrowth, bright flowers and interesting plants in the hedgerows, insects, and birds. My way took me under the railway bridge, too, and if I was lucky I would see the toy train thundering over.

I still took Rosemary for walks in her pram. Although it could be tiring, once again there was a lot to amuse me. The fields were infested with rabbits, and the lush giant undergrowth of the hedgerows teemed with animals that lived off them. Sometimes I would hear the desperate squealing of a rabbit caught by a stoat. I loved the wondrously tall roadside trees and the many birds that haunted them.

I was doing my needlework one day when I caught my arm on a protruding nail in my battered old desk and got a deep cut. They sent me for first aid to the friendly midwife who lived nearby, and the moment she saw who it was her eyes lit up. 'Not you again!' she laughed. 'What is it this time?'

Only a few short weeks before, I had run into the barbed-wire fence around the playground while racing after a ball, and she had had to put in some stitches. The pain was excruciating and my eyes overflowed with tears. More tears were already on the way in anticipation, but she laughed my fears away.

'No need for stitches this time, don't you worry. I'll just bandage you up and you'll soon heal. But if you're going to carry on like this I shall personally recommend you for the Military Medal for injuries sustained in the pursuit of education.'

On my way home from school it was my task to collect the milk from a nearby farm on the banks of a stream. Often I had to hang around waiting for the milking to be completed. A few yards from the cowshed was the usual huge dung heap, and a low wall ran along one side of it. Looking for something to amuse me, it occurred to me that the dung heap looked solid enough to hold my weight and it would be fun to take a running jump onto it from the wall. The farmer's wife stood frozen with disbelief at the cowshed door as I did so. And of course I sank in up to my knees and got stuck there. 'Whatever will you think of next,' she laughed.

Willing hands put planks across and helped pull me out, and what a mess I was. The cow-dung stuck to me like clay and I was hardly able to walk to the yard tap to try and wash it off. A brilliant idea occurred, however, and I got down into the stream with a borrowed scrubbing-brush. I washed my legs, socks and shoes until the smell was almost gone. I was soaking wet but clean. The milk was ready now and away I went, barefoot, the farmer and his wife laughing loudly behind me. I've always been one for getting into strange fixes.

When the cat's away, the mice will play, and the same thing applies to children and teachers. The headmaster had left us plenty of work to concentrate on, but the boys behind us girls decided to be disgusting instead. Two of them stood up and said, 'Look what we've got, girls.'

'And us too,' said others, in on the joke. There they stood, bold as brass, waving their willies at us. Disgusting, we thought, but brave and funny too, and we laughed and said, 'You wait, you dirty pigs. We'll tell Mr Jones. Put them away.' The rest of the boys, seeing our shocked faces, hastened to expose themselves also, and some got on top of their desks to improve the display.

The room was in uproar and back came Mr Jones in a fine temper to know what the noise was about. But by the time he got into the room, every single child was apparently hard at work — all, however, hiding radiant smiles.

Pubs are great places for tall tales. After a few pints you hear real-life stories that are not for repeating. The more serious-minded whisper them in the kitchen; the orators shout in the bar. As more pints go down, more skeletons emerge from their cupboards, accompanied by the caution, 'Not a word to anyone, mind!'

I heard many a sad or chilly tale, enough to make my hair stand on end. But I heard many a happy one, too, that gladdened the hearts of those who heard it and even brought tears sometimes. What must those men have thought next morning, though, when they remembered how the beer had talked?

Our isolated pub could be eerily quiet and sinister at night. Owls called in the high branches that encircled us, and bats were as numerous at night as crows in daylight. They could be heard squeaking as they flitted among the leaves.

The night skies, far from any streetlamps, could be spectacular with the great shimmering band of the Milky Way overhead and the flickering of innumerable individual stars. The great silence of the starry heavens set fire to our imaginations and brought to life the ancient beliefs of our ancestors.

The ty bach, being at the end of a long path under the orchard trees, could be a problem after two or three pints. Moonlight was a bonus because no artificial lighting was allowed for fear of attracting German aircraft. For those in a hurry, it was a crazy dash interrupted by collisions with trees—which brought out bright stars even when the sky was clouded—and which ended in, or was interrupted by, a resounding splash. Under the circumstances anywhere would do for a piss. After the bar was closed, you could hear splashing and farting all along the lane.

There were exciting nights when people brought along a variety of puzzles and tricks. Hours passed in the attempted unravelling of complicated mathematics. Pencils and paper were got out, and the more impatient frothed at the mouth with frustration. A local carpenter had a genius for mental arithmetic and could do in a fraction of a second calculations which baffled the scientists.

One night a farmer, recently bereaved, sat slumped over a table, drunker with grief than beer. His best milker had suddenly died. All who knew him pitied him, for she had been prolific with her milk and his concern over her loss was more than he could bear. He had spent days sitting up with this cow, comforting and nursing her through her final hours. Her failure to recover had hit him very hard. The beer had made matters worse rather than better.

He pounded the table with his fist until the glasses rang and shouted, 'Why, why, why, why?' There was no consoling him. They took him home at last, not so much out of kindness as out of fear of what he might do to himself if he had any more beer. His grief made him cry and cry.

Mari fach would never buy rabbits in the usual way, as a brace, but only by weight. One day a local character well known for his sharp dealing brought in a scruffy looking pair to sell or barter for beer. After looking doubtfully at them, she put them on the scales. Surprised at the discrepancy between their appearance and their apparent weight, she inspected them more closely and found a pound weight inside each of them.

'What's the meaning of this, then?' she asked, brandishing the weights in his face. *'Wel, dammo di!'* he exclaimed. 'The boy never told me he'd shot them with pound weights!'

He did not get his beer, and in his anger threw the skinny brace to the dogs, who chewed them up in no time at all. Mari left the weights on the windowsill for all to see the tricks that this not very lovable scoundrel got up to.

One day, a farm labourer attending the milking cows decided to let the bull in with them. This was a perfectly satisfactory arrangement—the bull certainly approved of it—until the time came to take the cows in for milking. Then the bull wanted to come, too. When the farmhand tried to shut the gate on him, the bull knocked him over. The farmhand rolled up close against the wall to protect himself, the raging animal all the time trying to toss or trample him.

He was sure his time had come—until a cockerel, enraged for some reason, flew full in the snorting bull's face, distracting him long enough for the man to escape with his life. That bull was put under restraint thereafter, and the hero of the day was allowed to live his natural life out to the full without fear of landing in the oven.

We had many an amusing moment during playtimes. One day the girls could not contain their laughter when they saw a dog mounting a bitch. He had overspent himself, and his back legs were so weak that he kept falling off. But so eager was he that he kept scrambling back. Finally he got stuck and away she walked, dragging him behind her.

The other children, envious of my life at the pub, were always asking if I drank beer. Not wishing to disappoint them, I insisted that I did. They looked at me as if I had committed a terrible crime and called out to the teacher. 'Miss, Miss, Beryl drinks!' She, however, knew me better than they did and was not impressed.

We had domestic science lessons, but I had no apron to wear. Cloth was on ration, so Mari fach made me one out of sacking. We all wore sacking aprons, in fact. Sacks had many uses among country people. Necessity is the mother of invention, especially in wartime, and they were used as body-warmers, shawls, leggings, and mattress covers. Farmers and their workers wore them on rainy days as anoraks are worn today.

As the pub had no running water, all supplies had to be jugged in from a pump down the road. We had no bathroom, and the lavatory was nothing more than a pit with a plank over it where in winter the up draughts froze your bum.

All drinking glasses had to be kept clean and clear. They were very thoroughly washed in hot, soapy water in a large vessel kept constantly warm on the fireside top. When the pub was full it was all hands to the pumps to maintain a supply of clean glasses on the bar shelves. Cleanliness was next to godliness for Mari, and any glass that was not crystal clear when it came out of the water had to go back again until it sparkled.

Baths were taken in a large, warmed bowl in front of a small fire in the outhouse shed, which had a heavy bolt on the inside to secure it against intruders. If by any chance the shed had not been pre-warmed, my teeth used to chatter. This roomy outhouse was also used for cooking and baking with calor-gas.

The back-kitchen was mainly for customers, though its fire and side hobs were used to bring pans to a slow boil or a simmer. In the colder corners, chickens and rabbits were hung, and legs of lamb and sides of bacon—this was to protect them from the rats.

The orchard was a minefield of rabbit-traps set to keep the rats down, but stray dogs and cats would often get caught in them and their cries of pain were very distressing, even more so as they were much better rat-catchers than all the traps put together.

As I lay on my bed at night, my thoughts still drifted back towards home. What was happening there, I wondered. I used to imagine myself back there, in my own bedroom or watching Mum at her housework. Then the bubble would burst and I would be back in the pub, pining for home and a loving mother. It seemed such a long time that we had been apart that I was afraid we would be strangers when we met again.

Mari and Bessi would have liked to adopt me, but they were sternly told that nobody was allowed to adopt an evacuee. All evacuees had to be returned eventually to their place of origin. I found myself in a terrible quandary, wanting to stay at the pub but at the same time loving Mum and wanting to be back with her. I still had no contact with her and no idea where she was or what was happening to her. The authorities pretended that they did not know where she was, and the billeting officer told me that he had no knowledge of her whereabouts. My letters were never returned, though—who was accepting them?

One morning I was so disturbed that I took a long walk to try and sort things out in my mind. The icy wind came whipping up the lane, there was a heavy ground frost, and I was devilishly cold. On the hill, the boulders looked as if they had woollen jumpers on. I was all alone; even the wandering sheep never gave me a second look.

When I got back I sat by the fire to thaw out. I told Mari where I had been and what was bothering me, and she listened very kindly to my childish chatter. I saw her face grimace with pain from her hurtful bladder complaint and put my arms around her. I hoped that my arms had a healing touch to ease her pain. There we sat, just the two of us. Before long she was telling me funny stories, we were both smiling, and the day seemed not so bad after all.

Chapter 11

I was walking in the garden one day when I heard someone call my name. It was Ben shouting over the wall between his smithy and the pub. 'Get me a glass of beer, *cariad*, and make sure the wife's not about. Here's the money.' I was not supposed to do this, and it had to be done carefully, without being seen. Ben's irritable wife kept a close eye on him, 'If Ben wants a drink,' she used to say, 'he can go to the horse trough!'

On very busy nights I was sent upstairs to my bedroom or to stay with Mari fach and Rosemary for company. Bessi wanted me out of the way in case I got trampled underfoot by the boisterous crowd of beer-swillers. Weekend nights were rip-roaring occasions when I found it completely impossible to sleep and would lay there listening to high-pitched voices raised in happy shouts and songs. The men enjoyed themselves as if tomorrow would never come. I supposed that one day I would get used to it and, like Mari fach and Rosemary, sleep through it all.

Eventually it would come to an end. Drunken voices, songs and shouting would die away down the lanes and I would drift off into a deep sleep until the Sunday morning birds woke me up. It was very delightful to be wakened to the sound of the birds and quiet movements down below where half the cleaning and tidying was already done. Bessi liked to have everything spick and span before the chapel-goers came by, all the glasses and jugs clean, all necessary supplies made up—and then relax over a nice bowl of tea and listen to the birdsong and the distant sound of hymns.

In their airy pews among the high branches, the undertaker crows were strangely quiet, their usual rowdy quarrellings temporarily suspended. Perhaps they too were listening to the hymns?

Although Sunday was supposed to be the day of rest, there was always plenty of work to be done, catching up on the chores for which there had not been time for in the bustle of a normal working day. Doors and windows stood wide open most of the morning so that anybody who happened to be passing could peep in. There was the smell of fresh air billowing through, and of disinfectant and polish.

Sometimes we would sit by the bar window and watch the congregation come pacing out of chapel, so much more briskly than they had walked in. Men would pause for a moment in the doorway to look cautiously around. What were their guilty consciences telling them, I wondered?

They would fumble in their jacket pockets, draw out the crumpled packet of fags, shove one into their mouths — then the sudden flash, the deep inhalation and slowly, so slowly, the fog billowed out of mouths and nostrils. What blessed relief. A few more urgent puffs, then, to catch up on lost nicotine and off they walked, so surrounded by fire and brimstone that I half expected to see horns sprouting from their heads and tridents in their horny hands.

'Fire-pigs' they were called by the non-smokers. Was there smoking in Heaven, I wondered. Did Jesus have the occasional fag? Did God?

What would those ghoul sisters of the vicarage have said if they could have seen me tucking in to a hearty Sunday dinner and thoroughly enjoying myself in a pub where their sour and bigoted religion never got a mention?

We saw some interesting sights from our vantage point in the bar. One Sunday a well-dressed couple walked up to the chapel door after the rest of the congregation had gone inside. After a quick look around to make sure that nobody was watching, the man embraced the woman and she heartily returned his passionate kisses. They were married people, both of them, but not to each other. Shocked, I saw him feel up inside the woman's dress. What had she got hidden up there that he was trying to find?'

Rosemary refused to have her meals with the others in the kitchen. She thought it was more fun to eat with me at the table by the window, where she could peep out to see whatever was going on. She ate more heartily with me in the bar. We were like two sisters.

I was never aware of any shortage of food here in the country, and rationing hardly seemed to exist. We had a delicious meal one Monday when Mari put a large cut of pork into the boiler and left it there to cook for several hours.

When it came to the table it was more tender than chicken and wonderfully tasty. The stock was used to pour over mashed potato or put in stews. There was fish for those who liked fish, and for those who did not there was beef, chicken, rabbit, mutton, pork, and bacon and eggs in abundance. Bread and butter, fine cakes, tarts, and pies were also readily available, but nothing was wasted. For me, who had known hunger and loneliness, it was like paradise.

From being one of the most unfortunate of evacuees, I was now one of the luckiest. Not only was I well fed, I was also surrounded by affection. Bessi and Mari fach looked on me as a daughter and a granddaughter. I was truly a Welsh-speaking girl now, at home and very happy.

One day, a commotion outside the smithy told us that the gypsies were back again. There they were, arguing furiously about why one of their ponies had gone lame and how best to treat it. 'The gathering of the clans,' said Bessi. It was uncanny how they managed to come together in one area at the same time from such distant and scattered places; some kind of telepathy seemed to operate.

Their women were an impressive sight in their long black ankle-length dresses. Their young girls were alluringly pretty in face and form, like porcelain dolls—unattainable, though, by any but gypsy men. They were kept, and kept themselves, strictly segregated within their tribes, and God help any outsider who tried to meddle with them.

The men were fine horsemen who carried with them knowledge handed down over the centuries. They were very superstitious and great story-tellers. They excelled at poaching, while their women went from door to door selling clothes-pegs and other things that they had made. They frightened the country women with their fortune-telling and occult powers.

The tribes had gathered on this occasion for the funeral of one of their powerful ones, and stopped in our neighbourhood to be together for a while before once again going their separate ways. There were mighty celebrations after the funeral, and many a man went swaying off drunk into the night.

When I went out early the next morning, I was shocked to find sleeping bodies slumped about the road and hedgerows. I ran back to tell Bessi about it. She took me roughly by the arm and said, 'You listen, now, and listen good to what I'm telling you, my dear girl. Stay safe in here and don't you be going out again until I tell you. Understand?'

'Yes.' I said, quite innocent of what she meant. There were things that a child was not supposed to see, and dangers too from men under the influence of drink. A few hours later it was as if the gypsies had never been; the tribes had migrated again. And I had learned on no account to meddle with people with such fearsome and uncertain tempers.

Travelling by bus in this remote countryside was an exciting business and could also be dangerous. As usual, it was the young people who caused the most trouble, especially for themselves. On one occasion two girl friends went by bus to the cinema in the nearest town. The film finished late, and they had to catch the last bus, which was already so full when they got to it that there was room left for only one standing passenger. The first girl had already got on, but got down again so that she could accompany her friend on the long walk home. But then her unscrupulous friend took advantage and jumped aboard. Off went the bus, leaving her friend miles from home and in the dark, a very frightening prospect.

The other girls on the bus, rightly disapproving of this treachery, ganged up against the traitorous friend, trapped her in a window seat, drowned out her cries for the conductor to stop when the bus reached her destination and caused her to be taken far out of her way. Justice was done; now she, like the friend she had betrayed, had a long, frightening walk home alone in the dark.

The conductors and drivers were a jolly lot; many a young countryman dreamed of getting a job on the buses where all the best-looking girls would chat with him for hours. I was too young to travel by myself, but I heard all kinds of stories about life on the buses: the dramas, the tensions, the lovers' quarrels, the singing of hymns and arias, and of course the terrible swearing. A war-time pantomime on wheels were the Welsh Fargo!

Bessi's husband had been a bus conductor and had some quite revolting tales to tell. In unguarded moments I heard things that I shouldn't, for example how, when the buses were crammed full, women and girls would find themselves being felt up by unseen fingers as they stood helpless in the crush.

I loved to help Mari fach with the cooking, for she was a wonderful cook and, for me, nearer to God than anyone I had ever known. Our meals were served at random times when the business of the bar permitted. The main meal was at some time in the evening, when, for example, we might have whole roasted rabbits on a large platter with two vegetables and lashings of brown gravy. Then, for pudding, apple dumplings and custard or — and this was food for the gods — rice pudding with a teaspoonful of jam on top.

Customers, made hungry by the savoury smells, would ask, 'Mari fach, is there any to spare?' And for special people there usually was. Mari always made plenty of food, and in her time fed doctors, cattle-dealers, schoolteachers and scientists.

Many a famous individual graced her back-kitchen: scientists from the nearby experimental establishments and top-notch officials of various kinds who preferred not to be known for what they were and what they were doing for the war effort. Important people used the pub as a kind of conference centre where they could have a drink and discuss confidential matters in private. Many a posh vehicle might have been seen parked outside, often chauffeur-driven and containing armed security guards.

Mari fach usually collected the flour from the cool cellar, but one day she was so busy that she asked me to get it for her. When I put the bowl into the half-full sack to scoop out the flour I was stupefied to see that the flour was on the move, seething all around it. I turned tail and ran back to tell her that there was something alive in the flour sack. She burst out laughing. Was it some joke she was playing on me? Her laughter was so contagious that I could not help joining in. 'They won't eat you,' she managed to say at last. 'It's only the old weevils. Quite harmless. Now, go back and get my flour, there's a good girl.'

I went back timidly and, with caution, my fingers tingling, hastily scooped out a bowlful and hurried back before I got bitten. Mari made no ado about mixing the flour into dough, and from it she made a whole lot of mouth-watering cakes, piping hot pancakes, Welsh cakes, and scones, all very tasty and nutritious. When the cakes were put on the table, though, I could not help inspecting them to see if there were any weevil holes.

Mari saw what I was up to and a smile came to her face as she said, 'Put that cake up to your ear, Beryl; perhaps you'll hear them chewing their way out!' I was silly enough to do as she said, realising too late that she was having me on. I had been revolted at the idea of eating creepie-crawlies, but the sight of pastries, pies, tarts, slab-cake, and bread soon converted me, and the next time she baked I helped mix the flour, weevils and all.

A favourite breakfast dish was Bread Tea, made by putting chunks of buttered bread in a bowl, pouring hot tea over them and adding milk and sugar to taste. Bowls were much more popular for tea-drinking than cups, and we had many of them in different colours and designs. Men generally preferred them because cups did not hold enough.

Mari had worn clogs all her life and never had any trouble with her feet. The only problem she suffered from was that affliction of the bladder, which sometimes caused her to say, 'I feel so tired, God rest my bones.' But she would add, 'But I have so much to thank Him for, with my loved ones around me, including you, my little girl.' I would get on my knees on the couch beside her and put my arms around her shoulders to comfort her. She liked me to do this, and she would look into my eyes and say, 'We're a pair, you and I. Both troubled, but I'm sure our ills will get better, just you wait and see.' She never stayed down in the dumps for long. Next day she would be a bundle of energy again, wanting to do everything herself. There was no stopping her when her dominant spirit was in the ascendant.

Among the many customers who came regularly to the pub were the two brothers, Dan and Wil. Dan was the introvert, quiet and mild-mannered; Wil was rowdy, fun-loving, full of song and never seemed to have a worry in the world. He loved the ditties of Harry Lauder, the Music Hall comic, and once he started singing them there was no more stopping him than there was his rusty old banger of a car.

'Keep right on to the end of the road,' he would warble. 'Keep right on to the end.' The vehicle had no brakes to speak of and ought to have been in the junkyard, but there was no such thing as the M.O.T. then. As he drove along the bumpy roads, parts of the vehicle kept falling off and the engine backfired and spluttered. When people heard him coming, they took refuge in gateways and behind trees, knowing that he would not be able to stop if they got in his way.

The way he stopped the car when he came to the pub was to drive it so close to the wall that the side scraped along and eventually worked as a brake. Many a wall bore his rusty signature; there was no paint at all on either side of the car. When he wanted to get on the road again, people had to help pull it clear of the wall.

When he couldn't find a wall to stop him, he used a hedge-bank. He had little or no road sense and was by no means always sober when driving — no breathalyser in those days — and went his merry way, doing the best he could with a steering system that did not work properly and all the time singing. 'Though the way be long, let your heart be strong ....' Everyone knew him as 'Wil Rust,' and how he had managed to survive so long without serious injury (to himself or anyone else) was a miracle.

Dan and Wil had a music room in the old farmhouse where they lived. It contained a grand piano left behind by a previous owner who could not afford, or could not be bothered, to move it, and a number of sheep. Dan would play the accompaniment to Wil's singing and the sheep would join in with a bleating chorus. The brothers spent more time in the pubs than on their sheep farm, leaving their distraught sister on the farm struggling to make both ends meet. All the money Dan and Wil could lay their hands on was spent on beer, so to get cash for housekeeping or to pay bills she would sell a sheep or two every so often.

Chapter 12

Many of the men who came to our pub were characters and behaved strangely. One man used to leave his wife and children crammed into the back of his van while he came in for a few pints. He would take packets of crisps and glasses of lemonade out to them to keep them quiet and then, before coming back into the bar, piss all over the van.

Another was the farmer who had lost a pig. He came into the bar brandishing a sharp-pointed butcher's knife and looking for the 'bastard' who had stolen from the back of his van the carcass of a pig that he was taking to flog on the black market. His language lit up the night! Hanging was too good for the thief — he ought to be tortured to hell and back. If he got hold of the man, he promised, he would chop him into quarters. He borrowed a flashlight and raged off into the night looking for his lost pig, but neither the pig nor the thief was ever found.

The passing convoys of American troops were manna from heaven to us children because the men threw out chocolate and packets of chewing-gum for us. Over-excited children took great risks collecting the sweets thrown from one lorry before the next speeding vehicle rumbled past. This cat-and-mouse game resulted in a number of near misses. Rosemary and I got our share and waved our thanks as the lorries roared away.

Bessi ruled her bar with a rod of iron. She had a strong personality and a penetrating voice, and she was afraid of nobody. She well knew that after a few pints of beer, men become argumentative, and that arguments lead to violence. She was quick to nip trouble in the bud with a sharp shout of 'Enough of that, now.' Everything would go quiet then, except for that small minority hell bent on annoying other people. 'You lot behave yourselves,' she would say, 'or I'll call the cops. You understand me now—this is your last warning.' This always worked because the men knew very well that the local police resented being called out to deal with drunks and that they would get roughed up.

'All right, Bessi,' they would say. 'All right.'

'Don't you "all right" me,' she would reply. 'Behave yourselves or you're out. Now!' Her flashing eyes made her so formidable that the toughest customers would walk off into the night to cool their tempers before coming back later to apologise.

Sometimes I got the rough side of her tongue, too. If she saw me in the passage she would shout, 'Get back to the kitchen right this second, where you're supposed to be. Go on, quickly now.' I always did as I was told without argument. Bessi felt better when Rosemary and I were safe aloft in our bedrooms; she was in control of the situation then.

Rosemary could be as stubborn as her mother, though, and sometimes refused to do as she was told. 'Get to that kitchen at once,' Bessi shouted at her one day, and suddenly, although it was none of my business, I found myself emotionally involved. 'Leave her alone,' I shouted, and I grabbed hold of Rosemary and locked us both into the parlour. I was not going to let Rosemary be bullied, even by her mother, and lost my temper on one side of the door while Bessi lost hers on the other. They got the door open at last, and took Rosemary away, but they couldn't make me let go of the door handle. I was so worked up that they would have had to break my fingers first.

A man was called to try and get me to release my hold but could not do it. He grinned at Bessi and said, 'You've got a problem here, Bessi. This girl's got a temper as bad as yours. When I look at her I'm looking at you. You'll have to compromise.'

Hearing the disturbance, Mari fach came to investigate. She beckoned with her finger and at once I ran to her, and off we went into the kitchen. 'Well, bless me!' Bessi exclaimed, breathing hard, and went off to the bar. Secretly, I think she was pleased to have found someone as headstrong as herself.

The dark cloud the war cast over everything made these years in many ways a carefree time. Conventional behaviour was suspended for the duration. Happy couples kissed, laughed, and danced in the dark roadway, determined to make the most of being young and in love, and to eat, drink, and be merry while they still could. Somewhere out of sight a land girl played a sad tune on her mouth-organ.

Then the spell was broken by a crash, a crunch, and the noise of scraping metal along the cemetery wall. Inquisitive customers hurried out with their tiny flashlights to see what had happened. They found dead rabbits all over the place: some drunk had crashed his van and made a run for it.

'Put that light out!' came a furious cry from the darkness. Men came back into the bar loaded with rabbits, and some hid a whole lot of them in the cemetery to sell for beer and tobacco money. There were more dead rabbits in the cemetery that night than dead people!

What was the use of crying? What was the point in worrying? Drink up, boys, that's the style, and take no thought for the morrow. Poaching was a profitable occupation, and often on quiet walks we'd see some man peering goggle-eyed through a hole in the hedge at grazing rabbits. What he was seeing was so many packets of fags, pints of beer, or glasses of whisky and rum!

Christmas arrived, a really hectic time for us. Decorations were made out of any colourful material that came to hand, yule logs were stacked high beside the fireplace, and a lamp with a red shade cast a warm glow over men's faces.

There were carol services, hymns, and vibrant wartime songs: Everybody had a concert in his heart. When our Christmas dinner was over, there was an unheard-of special treat—a box of crackers. They were a thing of such rare beauty from pre-war times, unobtainable now, that it seemed an act of vandalism to use them. We had one cracker each, and I did not pull mine but kept it as a special treasure. I would keep it forever.

In the midst of overpowering happiness my heart turned to home and to Mum, from whom there was still not a word. My thoughts flew out to her and tears welled up in my eyes 'Mum, Mum,' I whispered. 'Please write to me. Please. Just to let me know you're all right.'

Mari fach recognised my sadness and understood my tears and came to comfort my bitter thoughts. 'I know you want your mother, love, but she can't be here. Let me be a grandmother to you. Christmas is a time for remembering, but for enjoying, too.' I put my head on her shoulder and wept and between sobs whispered, 'Where is my Mum, Mari? Where is she?' She held me tight, hugging me and saying, 'There, now, what's all this? Tears? At Christmas time? Your mam will answer your letters, *cariad*, and she'll come to see you when the time is right for her to do so. No more tears, now. It's not like you to worry.'

The others looked on without a word; they knew that I did not get any letters from home. In bed that night, by the light of my stump of flickering candle in whose flame I seemed to see her face, I talked to Mum. 'Dear Mum, I hope your Christmas was as good as mine and with all my heart I hope you're happy and well. Are you thinking of me? So much time has passed since we saw one another — will we be strangers when we meet again? What will we have to say to one another?' I bit my pillow in my grief and my voice was muffled as I spoke into it, 'Mum, what's happened to you?' I blew out the candle. It had been a long day's celebration. Time to sleep now.

At long last I was sleeping at night without bad dreams, thanks to the tender loving care of Mari fach and Bessi. I had grown used to the rowdy night noises of the pub and had no difficulty in dropping off to a deep and lovely night of unbroken slumber. It was a miracle.

One morning I woke early feeling that things were not us they should be. Everything was so strangely silent. Looking out of my window I saw that it had snowed heavily during the night. I sneaked down and went out to be the first person to make footprints in the new white carpet. Everything in the world seemed to possess eternal loveliness, but the wind blew cold, the flakes still drove down, and soon the roads would be blocked by drifts. I crept up to my still warm bed, fell back into dreamless sleep, and woke late.

To my surprise I found trenches in the deep snow where people had ploughed through, forcing their way to work on ice-cold feet. Soon the heavy military convoys were ploughing their way through, clearing a path for the bus.

This bad weather reduced trade at the pub for a while, and we had long drowsy evenings in an almost empty kitchen with the yule-log fire sending shadows flickering. The light was out and I sat eating a juicy apple and trying to read by firelight. Life was wonderful in those moments.

The pub radio was not much used because its constant reports of death and disaster upset the customers. They had, after all, come here to escape all that, if only for a few hours. War news affected different people in different ways. Some men liked to think themselves expert strategists, and sharp arguments that nobody could possibly win would break out and end in fist-fights. What the ears don't hear, nobody can argue about, so Bessi switched the radio off and left it that way.

Men in uniform drank as if there was no tomorrow. Their robust songs shook the pub to its very foundations. Night after night, week after week they bellowed them out. It was a wonder their trumpeting did not bring it down about our ears like the walls of Jericho. 'We'll meet again,' they sang, 'don't know where, don't know when, but I know we'll meet again some sunny day ...' and 'There'll be bluebirds over the white cliffs of Dover tomorrow, just you wait and see ….' Far from home, their lives in danger, separated from sweethearts, wives, children, they found in beer the blood of life and in song the echoes of the soul. Pubs were cages for the aching human heart.

I took Rosemary, well wrapped up and buried under her pram covers, for walks along the frosty lanes. To get my circulation going, I raced along and she woke up and giggled with delight as we twisted, turned, slipped and humped along. I must have broken all records for the mile-and-a-quarter pram race, out and back again. Then it was lovely to de-frost again in the warm air of the pub.

Men and women alike were determined to get as much out of life as they could. The evil rabbit-trappers had more than they needed for just beer and baccy, but there were women who knew how to separate them from their spare cash. Everywhere couples romanced away the night and the war.

On my solitary walks, though, I heard the squeals and pitiful whimpering of snared animals and thought what terrible cruelty men inflicted just for a lungful of smoke and a bellyful of firewater. In the bar at night I would fancy I saw, in the smoke that rose over the revellers' heads, apparitions of the birds, animals, and fish they had slaughtered. If only rabbits could trap men, gut them and bake them in a crusted pie dish, let them steam in their own blood, and make them into Poacher's Pie.

Evenings in the pub, there were often drunken and rowdy disagreements between the jolly American soldiers and the loud-mouthed and braggart gypsies. They would be sent out into the roadway to settle their differences, in total darkness. It was the blind fighting the blind. The American soldiers were taller and stronger, and quieter, and they silenced the gypsies. The good-hearted GIs were always the proud victors, and they laughed and joked about it. We all did, too.

I was never allowed alone near any man, Mari and Bessi saw to that. No man was allowed to chat me up — my innocence was plain to see.

On my way home with the milk one day I noticed a great flock of crows circling over the pub. 'Caw, caw, caw,' they went, making a terrific fuss. I understood at once what they were really saying. 'Cawl, cawl, cawl,' was what they meant, and they were right, there was cawl, soup-stew, my favourite, for supper.

That night I looked out of my window at the moon, that poor heavenly body blamed for so many of the world's miseries. Its unseen influence struck fear and caused physical and mental weakness in man and beast. Crazy people used to spit at it and shout, 'That Man-in-the-Moon needs a black eye.'

Under the moon the cemetery, that safe haven for lovers, was bathed in its eerie glow. A drunken lover betrayed his presence and activity by shouting, 'If that bloody moon don't go down soon I'll bloody strangle it, that's what!' Nobody was to see what he was up to among the headstones.

There was one soldier so well known for his regular manoeuvres in the cemetery that they called him 'Tombstone Dic!'

Chapter 13

Some weekends Rosemary and I used to catch the Welsh Fargo buses for a visit to her Aunt Annie, who lived in a remote farm cottage up in the mountains. It was so quiet up there you could hear the grass grow under your feet. At Aunt Annie's farm I tasted whinberry pie for the first time. It was ambrosia to me, food for the gods, and I could have eaten the whole pie myself in a wonder mouth of sheer pleasure.

Aunt Annie took us up into the wild hills to pick the precious whinberrics before sheep ate the lot. 'Who taught you to make whinberry pie?' I asked, and she said, 'Many years ago, when I was a young girl like you, playing and wandering among these hills, some fairies invited me to play with them. They took me to their home and taught me how to make fairy pies. This cottage was built inside a fairy ring. Their ovens are still there under the foundations, and sometimes at night you can hear them snoring.'

One quiet evening there was a slight earth-tremor that rattled the crockery on the dresser. 'It's all right,' Aunt Annie said. 'It's only the little people dancing. They do it all the time, day or night: our time has no meaning for them.' Aunt Annie's cottage was a secret wonderland for Rosemary and me. We couldn't wait to go back there, though this depended on the weather. The mountain was no place to be when the weather was bad.

I still have the most wonderful memories of Aunt Annie and her farm. We were very fond of her and called her 'Auntie Magic.' She accepted me as Rosemary's sister, and there was a strong bond between us. She promised to take us to the mysterious place where the fairies lived, though I was afraid they would shrink us to their own size. The visits to Aunt Annie are a very important part of my memories of those war-torn years during which I grew from childhood to maturity. I often wish that I could re-live them.

Familiarity breeds contempt, they say. Sometimes I got above myself and dared to argue with my good friend Bessi. 'I'll be glad to go home!' I said, in the heat of the moment, though I knew even then that I didn't mean it but was only speaking out of spite and a desire to hurt her. She had more sense, however, than to be taken in by my immature behaviour.

'Now, Beryl,' she would say, 'don't you speak to me like that. This is your home and always will be. Just remember that.' When my quick hot temper had cooled, I would suffer deep pangs of guilt for speaking so horribly to her and be anxious to atone for my ill-natured behaviour. I would swallow my pride and go back to her and apologise most sincerely. She would embrace me and I would feel very much better.

The war had become the normal state of affairs. I had more or less come to take it for granted that it would go on forever and I would always be an evacuee. I was living in a fool's paradise.

On May 7, 1945, the war ended. And so, in the midst of all the wild celebrations, did my happy life, What was going to happen to me? Who was I, even? I no longer belonged to this land in which I had been so terribly unhappy and then so very fortunate.

At school my classmates would say, 'It won't be long now before you'll be going home.' But the very idea frightened the life out of me. For a time, however, the happy routine of my life went smoothly on. It could not last.

I was seated at my desk one day when the headmaster brought two uniformed women into the classroom. I thought at first they were school inspectors. But then he looked at me in a way that made my heart turn over and said, 'Beryl, will you come with us, please.' My curious classmates whispered, 'Whatever have you done, Beryl fach?'

We went into the tiny staffroom and I was introduced to the two hard-faced women. They belonged to the East Coast Authority and had come to break some bad news to me. 'Sit down, please,' said one of them, in an embarrassed tone. There was a long pause while she fumbled for words. Then she said. 'You understand that you have to go back to your home-town, don't you?'

'I don't want to go back,' I said. 'Do you understand?'

'We do understand,' said the other one, 'that you are very happy here and settled, but you must go back. That is the law.'

I let them continue, not hearing nor understanding what they were saying, until, 'We have some terrible news for you. Your mother is dead.'

The headmaster broke in hastily. 'Are you all right, Beryl?'

Dazed, I heard the voice continue. 'She was run over by an army lorry and killed instantly. We are very sorry.'

But she was not sorry at all, for she went on to quote from her handbook of regulations, 'All evacuee children must be returned to the towns of their departure ....'

She was still quoting regulations when I shouted, 'I haven't got a home or a mother any more. I don't want to go back. I haven't even got any family there. I want to stay here. Why can't I stay here?'

'I'm sorry, child,' came the reply. 'We are only doing our duty.'

'Where are my brother and sister?' I asked. 'Are they dead too?' Those silly women could tell me nothing. They had come all this distance without any answers to the most obvious questions—as if their journey had just been an excuse for some sightseeing in the country.

'We have no idea of the whereabouts of your family,' was the reply.

I could neither think nor speak any more. The one thought kept going round and round in my brain: 'Your mother is dead. Mum is dead. Mum is dead.'

I got back to my class somehow, and the other children pestered me with questions. 'My mum's dead.'

I replied. 'She was killed by an army lorry.' My classmates fell silent, which upset me even more. Then the headmaster came in and asked, 'Would you like to go home now, Beryl?'

'No, thank you, sir,' I said, 'I'd rather stay in class. I've got so many things to think about.' So he let me stay there, and everybody was kind and gentle with me, and I did not know how I was going to tell Bessi and Mari fach. I wanted to run away and hide.

After school I made my way back to the pub like a dog that has been whipped. I was overwhelmed with guilt, I felt that nobody wanted me or cared about me. How could I look them in the face?

When I got there I crept up to my room and fell on my bed in floods of tears. I pulled the bedclothes over my head and took refuge in the black night of my thoughts. I had thought myself unhappy at the vicarage, but that was nothing compared to my feelings now. All I wanted was for someone to help me die. I had no hope and nothing whatever to live for.

It was dear Mari fach who came to comfort me. She sat by me on the bed and put her gentle arms about me. I sat up to cuddle her as closely as I could. I never wanted to let her go. The tears poured from my eyes. Her voice when she spoke was calm and gentle. 'I know,' she said 'I know all about it, *cariad*.'

Between sobs I said, 'I don't know what I've done. Why does everything hurtful happen to me and there's nothing I can do to stop it? They won't let me stay with you. I've lost my own family and now I'm going to lose you. I wish I'd stayed where I was and been blown up in an air raid. I'd rather die than go away from here.'

Mari was crying too. 'Try not to fret, love,' she said. 'I shall stay with you wherever you are. Try to put those dreadful thoughts out of your mind. Wherever you go, wherever you go, you will always be one of our family. We know how you feel, we understand it very well, and we want to share your sorrows and help you in any way we can. Come on down now and have your tea.'

'All right,' I managed to say. 'Just give me a minute or two.'

I went down. I washed my face in cold water. I had my tea and felt a little better for it, and fortunately there was nobody around to make me feel embarrassed. After a while I managed to behave more or less as if nothing had happened, but the uncertainty was dreadful.

The following morning, Mari fach and Bessi were arguing with the billeting officer and trying, once again, to adopt me. They had tried before, not long after I had been transferred to them, but in vain. The

East Coast Authority had not wanted to know. All they cared about was the letter of the regulations: my personal circumstances meant nothing to them. I was alone and stricken with grief while the rest of the world danced around me, celebrating the end of the war.

I seemed to have been born unto trouble as the sparks fly upwards, a kind of scapegoat whose only purpose in life was to suffer. Tragedy should have been my name. Those damned officials had never told me the truth until the worst possible moment. Mum had been dead for years, yet somebody had received my letters. What had been done with them? Where was she buried?

Two years previously Mari and Bessi had attempted to adopt me and those officials had known then that mum was dead and I was an orphan, yet still they refused me the chance of a happy family life. It was inhuman.

I tried to settle back into the routine of the life of the pub, but my thoughts were dogged by doubt. I knew it was only a matter of time before I would be taken away. The notification soon arrived, and we all wept together. My feelings were tearing me to pieces. I could not sleep at night. Saying goodbye to my friends was a torture to me.

The last day came. The billeting officer arrived in his car. I did not want to take anything but the clothes I stood up in, but faithful Mari fach had packed all my belongings for me. Luckily, Rosemary was asleep when the time came; it would have been very hard to leave without her; she was my little girl and always would be. I crept upstairs to see her for the last time, sleeping peacefully, and my tears wet her warm face as I bent to kiss her goodbye, leaving a tiny flower on her pillow.

Like the condemned criminal on the way to the gallows, I had nothing to say.

Bessi, Mari fach, and I gathered in one last heart-breaking embrace. The blackbird's song rang out clearer than ever through the clear morning air, a haunting requiem for the heart that had died within me.

History had repeated itself. I had been evacuated against my will from a happy home to fend for myself among strangers. I had found happiness again, and a loving family. Now, a Welsh-speaking stranger, I was being evacuated again to fend for myself again among new strangers. I got into the car. The blackbird's song ceased. The hearse drove away.

Chapter 14

I was emotionally stunned. My eyes blurred with tears at the prospect of losing my only true Welsh 'home.' I loved it beyond words. My enchanted home was no more, along with my lovely Welsh carers—Mari fach, her daughter Bessi, and little Rosemary.

'Good-bye and God bless you all!'

My Dartford home in Kent was also no more, and I had no idea of what had become of my brother and sister.

Sitting in the car, I felt like a wounded rabbit caught in a trap, and all I wanted to do was jump out of the car and run all the way back to Mari fach and Bessi. A need to belong became an overpowering force imprinted in my mind.

We eventually arrived at Herne Bay in Kent, where I was to attend a teaching hospital for young girls wishing to become children's nurses. Seeing the dirty and claustrophobic streets filled me with dread of what was to come. Soon, things proved difficult. I couldn't get on with the English students, who were rough and insolent, with their mouthy and insulting behaviour. In the quiet evenings, *hiraeth,* the Welsh word that means a longing for one's home or past, felt like a lead weight inside me.

My classmates treated me like a country bumpkin and their unkind words hurt, until enough was more than enough. I asked my aunty if I could stay with her. She agreed, as she had a small bedroom for me. But within a few days I realized I had leapt from the frying pan into the fire.

I soon found employment at a biscuit factory for £1-0-3 pence a week. But my aunty demanded that I hand my wage packet over to her unopened. I was not allowed a few pence to buy tea, toast, and jam at morning tea break. So without her knowing, I used my own money.

One day I went to visit my grandmother. Before the war I was her favorite, but this time a verbal bomb shell exploded in my face. I stood in all innocence at her front door while her daughters blocked my way. The verbal heat coming from her kitchen was full of hostility. 'Send that Welsh bitch away from my door! I have no intention of meeting her.' She threw flames of hatred at my Welsh accent. I was no longer one of their family; to her daughters, I was a 'tramp child' and no relation of theirs.

Hurt and red-faced, I walked away like a cowering dog. My aunty was just as bad, always cold-hearted and blunt when she talked to me. She smoked a lot and drank. She was no friend, and she let me know it.

Coming home from work one day, I found that my shoulder bag, which I had hidden behind my overcoat that was hanging on the back of my bedroom door, was missing. All my worldly cash was inside it. When I asked her about the bag, she flew into a rage. 'Are you calling me a thief in my own home? You shall be taken out of this house tomorrow. The Welfare people will take you away!'

Sure enough, a Welfare woman was at the door the next day and took me by train to the Church Army Hostel in Gloucester, far away. The barefaced lies my aunty must have told about me I never learned. And I never had my bag or money back.

Robbed and thrown to the wolves, I was a stranger in an alien environment. I never knew loneliness could be so heart-breaking. But I managed to survive, despite the humorless people around me, who always seemed to be at odds with me. I was destitute and I had to learn fast how to live on meagre wages.

Different jobs came and went. My fears and lack of confidence always made them difficult, and the curses and swearing I heard were mind-blowing to me. I was earning just enough to pay my lodging. But my troubled heart was back in Wales.

I eventually found a job at Top Dogs, a Breakliners Company, in Bristol at £3 and a few pennies a week. At last I had enough money to pay my lodgings at £1 30 per week and keep the rest to myself. By careful saving, I figured I could take a holiday back to Wales. I rejoiced at the thought that I might one day be home among my own kind.

On my third yearly visit, I met two sisters who told me I could stay with them, paying their mother £1 30 per week. There, on a hot Sunday afternoon, I was having a farmhouse tea when I met someone who would change my life forever. A few local lads came in, and one looked at me and jokingly remarked, 'You'll do!'

I took to him and we dated and became good friends. I decided to leave Bristol and take a job with the Black Lion Hotel in Cardigan for £3 a week. His name was Idris Mathias, and he was a postman who delighted in researching the Teifi River fisheries and spinning local ghost tales. At the time we met, he was spending most of his evenings drinking in the pubs. He was broke, and I was just as bad off, but even so we decided to get married without a penny between us.

When the registrar found out that I was a few months off my 21st birthday, which was the legal age for girls to marry then, he hesitated. But since I had no next of kin, he decided to go ahead and marry us. It was on a Saturday in December 1950. We went to live with Idris's father and two sisters, Mona and Millie.

He gave up drinking and passed his wage packet to me unopened. He intensified his research into the Teifi River fisheries. After long years of hard, solid work, the result was an amazing map, hand-coloured and nearly 60 feet long. They called him the 'Map Man', and even though I had just a part in it, they called me the 'Map Lady.' The map is now a local treasure and in my keeping.

We have five fine children, three boys and two girls, all grown up and grandparents themselves. We live in Cardigan Town, Ceredigion, not far from the Penybryn Arms pub, where once so long ago I was a war evacuee. A son and a daughter live in Cilgerran, and their children attended Cilgerran School, where I went to school in the 1940s.

We have been happily married for 63 years.

Printed in Great Britain
by Amazon